THE HOUSE CHURCH

THE HOUSE CHURCH

PHILIP and PHOEBE ANDERSON

Abingdon Press
Nashville   New York

THE HOUSE CHURCH

Copyright © 1975 by Abingdon Press

Library of Congress Cataloging in Publication Data

ANDERSON, Philip A. The house church. Bibliography: p. 1.
House churches. I. Anderson, Phoebe M., joint author. II. Title.
BV601.85.A5   254'.6   74-19144

ISBN 0-687-17437-6

Scripture quotations are from the Revised Standard Version of the Bible, copyrighted 1946, 1952, and 1971, by the Division of Christian Education, National Council of Churches, and are used by permission.

In this book *he, him,* and *his* are used in the established sense, when appropriate, as pronouns of the common gender to include the male and the female. Since gender is a category of grammar rather than sex, the use of the already existing distinction is made solely in the interest of clarity and economy of language.

MANUFACTURED BY THE PARTHENON PRESS AT
NASHVILLE, TENNESSEE, UNITED STATES OF AMERICA

Dedication

To all the house church members
whose lives have touched ours,
whose stories have increased our
sensitivities, and whose love has
supported our own journeys.

Introduction

The house church process described in this book holds great promise as a response to the crises in the churches. The loss of membership and resources, uncertainty about the theology and purpose of the church, evidence that church members are not automatically more loving than nonchurch members (indeed, some studies show the very opposite to be true), disillusionment with social action, the inadequacy of care for members, and the nagging feeling on the part of many that the church is not living up to its profession are widespread problems of Protestant, Roman Catholic, and Jewish congregations. The house church, as we have experienced it and have here detailed it, is one answer to these problems. We have attempted to show that persons can create and participate in a loving, caring community beyond any they have known, given the opportunity and the leadership. Small, face-to-face groups meeting over weekends or in extended periods of time can get past the superficiality and unimportance of much of what they have heretofore experienced in churches to relationships of depth and meaning and concern.

The house church process described in this book is also a response to some of the crises in the culture: the rootlessness produced by a high mobility rate, the loneliness and isolation of persons, the meaninglessness of existence, the wistful search for personal growth and relevance, the estrangements in human relationships and families, the dissolution of marriages, the need for significant belonging. Persons who become members of a house church find that their loneliness and isolation are greatly reduced, that their lives take on new meaning and purpose, that they can grow through estrangements and fragmentations toward wholeness and oneness to new depths of belonging. In the popular language of the day, they can get themselves together, both within themselves and in their relationships.

There are currently many resources for the work of the church. These come primarily from the fields of humanistic psychology. Although we have not used the jargon or particular language from any field or discipline, we are nevertheless clearly indebted to much of the theory and practice of Gestalt therapy, psychosynthesis, bioenergetics, transactional analysis, group dynamics, meditation, mysticism, and Eastern religions. We acknowledge our reliance upon the thought of many men and women in these fields and are grateful to them. The church has always used the resources emerging in the culture to communicate the Good News. Many of the current developments are fads and will pass away within a decade or two. Whatever is found to be helpful to persons, to promote wholeness, to enhance loving and caring will remain. Call it spiritual, mystical, religious, transcendent, flower power, or of the nature of God, no matter. What is authentic will remain. What is merely flashy or opportune or popular will pass away.

The loving, accepting, authentic experiences of the house church are not bound by age, sex, national region, or culture. During our work on the staff of the Christian Counseling Center in

Vellore, India, we confirmed what we had already strongly be-lieved: that love, fear, anger, and pain are universal, that ambiva-lences and fragmentations and estrangements are disabling, and that acceptance, forgiveness, and reconciliation are longings of the human spirit no matter what its condition or culture. We have had no experiences that deny these truths. Old and young, men and women, northerners, southerners, easterners, and westerners within the church and without it want meaning, belonging, and inner peace for their lives. An ongoing house church can offer these experiences to its members.

Now to a different concern, about personal pronouns, *he* and *she*. The English language uses the masculine form of the per-sonal pronoun in the singular (he, his, him) to refer to both male and female persons. We have sought diligently for an alternative to this usage. We searched the linguistic origins of English and could find no acceptable Old English form. We devised new pronouns (sheu, shir, shim), but many of our friends objected to their sound and form. In the end we recast many of our sentences to eliminate the third person singular masculine pronoun. But we are not wholly satisfied with the result, and so we have accepted, with some reluctance, the practice of Abingdon Press in this matter (see note). The women's movement may succeed in chang-ing this usage. We want to be on record as urging that change and continuing to do all we can to support it.

We are grateful to all the persons who have participated in house churches with us across the country, to our colleagues, and to our students. Several colleagues who have been pilgrims with us in the search for authentic church life have read the manuscript and made significant suggestions for its improvement. We value their help, their encouragement and support. We want especially to extend our love, gratitude, and shalom to Elizabeth and Jerry Jud, May and Arthur Foster, Carol and Perry Le Fevre; Jan and Bob Stickney. We want also to thank Gertrude and Ray Johanson, the United Church Board for Homeland Ministries, and the Chicago Theological Seminary who have enabled house church experiencing with their time, space and resources. Finally, we want to say thanks to Jo Davis, our longtime friend and secretary who typed many drafts of this manuscript and whose patience, buoyancy, and love have always sustained us.

Also we should add that all identifying names and places have been changed to protect the privacy of the participants throughout this book.

PHOEBE AND PHIL ANDERSON
January, 1975

Contents

Part 1
The House Church — What It Is and Why

1. A House Church Is Born

One Friday night in October, sixteen persons associated with the Parker Community Church gathered in the family room of the home of one of the sixteen, ready to participate in a new, to us, experience of churchmanship—the house church. We were both young adults and senior citizens; men and women; married, single, divorced, separated; longtime church members; friends of the members; friends of the friends; and even a few persons unrelated to the church in any way. The family room was furnished with pillows and bean bag chairs which were moved about for comfort. Everyone was sitting almost on the floor. Judging by the small talk at the beginning and the casual attire, we, the participants, were expecting to find new friends as informal as we were. The house church was scheduled to meet from Friday night until Sunday afternoon, with time out for sleeping, of course, which is as long as the majority of church going adults spend in the pews participating in Sunday morning worship for a year!

The leader was a person from outside the community, a man who had spent many years of his life as a pastoral counselor and a leader of small groups. The minister of the Parker Church had asked him to provide the beginning leadership in the formation of a house church. Some of us knew him; most did not.

He said a few words about the intention of the house church to become a loving community, a cultural island for forty-four hours apart from the interruptions, pressures, and expectations of "back home"; about the relation of mind and body and spirit; about the inability of most of us to give words to our feelings as well as to our ideas.

"Let's begin by introducing ourselves to the group. First, say your name, then say what you are aware of, then repeat your name as many times as you wish until it feels and sounds right in this house church. The group will respond by saying your name three times, trying to catch how you said it, as a kind of litany of recognition. I'll start. I'm Jim, and I'm a little nervous and very hopeful. Jim, Jim, Jim."

Sixteen persons had sixteen different names, but not sixteen different feelings. Some were fearful, tense, apprehensive, reluctant; some were tired and wished they were home, or at least not in the group; some were exhilarated, greatly anticipating something. After we had gone around the circle, said our names and heard them, and reported our feelings, the fearful and the tired ones were less so, and the anticipating ones were more so. The tensions had decreased a notch.

We took a blind walk with partners, and, then, once again in our circle, focused our thinking and feeling on issues of trust and responsibility. These seemed to be pretty dependable people; the tensions decreased another notch. We held several five-minute conversations with one other person, a different person for each conversation, on a variety of subjects which the leader provided for us: What do you do with your anger? Tell your partner about the parent you have the greatest problem with. Share an experience of grief. (We held each other's hands and closed our eyes as we talked.) Brag about your strengths. How do you show your love? Relate an early childhood memory. What do you like to do for fun? As one of our conversations we had a loud, noisy, laughing time trying to force open each other's tightly closed fist. The leader said the closed fist and the open hand are symbols of how he, and we, will function in the house church. All of us are in control of our own lives. We can open them or close them; no one is going to force us to do or say or act in any way we are not prepared to do. That was comforting. The tensions decreased another notch.

At the close of the conversations, we knew half the group quite well, for we had talked with them. We did not know the persons in our own half as well. The leader assigned each half the task of devising some symbol—movement, song, game—which could be done with the other half and which would symbolize our wholeness, our unity. One group created a version of the "Farmer in the Dell"; the other taught us all a singing circle dance. The evening ended in song and dance and hilarity. And food. We gathered around on our floor pillows again, drinking coffee and tea, and eating apples and cookies.

"Before we break for the night, let's go around our circle once again expressing what we are aware of now," the leader said.

The awareness of sixteen persons had changed dramatically from the first time around, three hours before. Some reported feeling relaxed and at ease; some were surprised at how fast the time had gone; some said they felt closer to some individuals in our group than to almost everyone back home; some were still curious about the morrow, but their anxiety had been greatly reduced; some were completely tired out and ready for bed.

So the evening ended. Clearly the tensions had been lowered several notches.

Saturday morning after breakfast, the leader gave each person a large sheet of drawing paper, 18″ X 24″, with instructions to make a picture having four parts.

   a) Your life as it is now.

  b) Your life as you'd like it to be.
  c) What's blocking you?
  d) What do you need to overcome the block?

He assured us that drawing skill was not needed. We could use whatever color or colors we wanted, could create any symbol or image or picture which came to mind.

Half an hour later everyone was finished, and we gathered again in our circle.

"Before we share our pictures with one another, I need to explain our ground rules. These are *dos* and *don'ts* which much experience has shown to be helpful." The leader wrote four don'ts on a flip chart before us, amplifying and illustrating the points in turn.

  1. No judgment. Each person is his own best judge. "Judge not, that ye be not judged."

  2. No interpretation. Analyses, explanations and "why" questions are usually not very helpful.

  3. No problem-solving. We never know enough to solve another person's problems. Each person can solve his own once he finds his blocks and his strengths.

  4. No helping. We are not here to rescue a person from his situation. Each person needs a human community in which he can experience his life fully without being cajoled, hushed up, "saved," or bailed out.

A man in the group who, we later learned, had spent all his adult life as a counselor responded quickly and with considerable feeling, "What's left? You've just knocked the props out from under the helping professions. What is a clergyman to do, for instance?"

We laughed, a little nervously. All of us were thinking the same thing.

"You're right about much of the practice of the helping professions. In fact, most of us acting as good neighbors, caring friends, or supportive colleagues act in these ways. So I've made another poster, stating the positives." He made another page on the flip chart in much the same way as he had done with the first.

1. Be present. Let your presence be known. Communicate your care and your love by word and by touch. No one cries alone in this house church.

2. Accept. God has accepted each of us with our mistakes and our inadequacies. In Christ's name, let us accept one another.

3. Listen. Hear one another's words *and* the feelings behind the words: pain, anger, grief, joy, longing, love, etc. Respond to the words and the feelings.

4. Encourage and support. Offer persons ways of working through their blocks, enabling them to find their own interpretations and solutions.

Most Important of All

Each person tells his own story. No one tells another's.

The leader paid particular attention to the last injunction. "Confidentiality must be preserved on this cultural island. You may, of course, tell anyone *your* story and *your* experience, but do not tell anyone else's. In nearly a decade of work with people in house churches across this nation, I have never heard of one case of the confidence and trust established here being violated."

That was comforting to hear.

"Who wants to share his or her picture with us?"

Clarence responded immediately. He was a middle-aged businessman, anxious to get the ball rolling, he said. His first image (where I am now) was filled with representations of his many responsibilities: family, church, community, business. The telephone stood out, large and demanding. The second image (where I would like to be) was a mountain scene. It was peaceful and quiet with a cabin and a path to it and trees all around. The third image (what's blocking me) was a huge stone labeled Responsibilities which lay across his path in such a way that he could not go around it. The fourth image (what do I need to overcome the block) was dollar signs and clocks, representing money and time.

We listened, asked a few questions of clarification and sat silent, many of us knowing and feeling how heavy and burdensome responsibilities do become and not knowing how we could help Clarence manage his, if indeed we could.

"Clarence, where in your body do you carry all these responsibilities?" the leader asked.

"In my back," he answered immediately.

"Have you ever let others support you?" Clarence didn't know what the leader meant. "We can't solve all these problems for you, but we can let you experience another way to feel for awhile. Will you let us carry you for a few moments, let go of the control you have of your mind, body, and emotions, just relax and let go?"

The proposal seemed a little foolish, and no one knew quite what to do or what to expect, but Clarence was quite willing to go along with it. At the leader's directions he lay down on his back in the middle of the circle, we put our hands and arms under him and lifted him up and rocked him back and forth for several minutes. Gradually he was able to relax. The muscles of his arms and legs and neck and face let go, and he became quite heavy. Slowly and carefully we lowered him to the rug and, at a signal from the leader, placed our hands on him. Thirty warm hands from head to toe offered him our support and strength in carrying his heavy, heavy load of responsibility.

Clarence opened his eyes. "What a trip! I hated for it to end. I began to feel so light and free. For heaven's sake! My back feels better! How can that be?"

We were as astonished as Clarence, for we had done nothing but hold him and rock him, and he had done nothing but let us hold him while he relaxed, and the back tensions diminished. The leader had said there is a unity of mind and body and that the body has much wisdom. Is this what he meant?

The minister of the group, Paul, then wanted to share his picture. In the first section (where I am now) he pictured himself high in a tower of a splendid castle. A large crowd of people milled around in front of the castle, looking for something or someone. The minister imprisoned in his tower was calling "Help!" through a window. No one heard him.

The second part (where I'd like to be) was a pleasant scene in a garden with many people gathered around an old country inn named Inn of the First Happiness. The scene was one of joy and peace and belonging.

The third representation (what's blocking me) was a wall composed of many bricks labeled fear, unrealism, choices, church, roles, resentment, image, insecurity, pride, blaming others, system. Over the top of the wall, two hands and the top half of a head were barely visible. He was peering over the top.

The fourth image (what do I need to overcome the block) had two words, *courage* and *commitment,* leading into some footsteps which led to the Inn of the First Happiness.

The leader asked Paul to stand on a high stool, way above the house church members on the floor below, to try to feel his isolation and loneliness. Paul began to speak.

"I feel separated and isolated and very lonely. I feel strange. Everyone is looking at me as if I'm different." He laughed wryly. "Ha, ha! I guess I am different. I'm up here and everyone else is down there. I can't see anyone's eyes very clearly, I'm too far away. I can't touch anyone, I'm too far away. I want to come down and get close to others, but that is scary. This is just the way it is with me, and those blocks are still in my wall. I would like to blame all of you for putting me up here, but I know I got up here myself."

The leader encouraged Paul to become even more aware of himself up there in his "tower." He closed his eyes for what seemed like a long time. When he opened them and looked around again, his eyes began to get moist, his body trembled, and he said, "I want to get out of this tower and join all of you, but I'm not ready yet. I've got to face some of my blocks." With that he sat down on his chair tower and put his head in his hands.

Several members of the group started forward to comfort him, but they were waved back by the leader. "We are all here for Paul. But he must decide to come down from his tower or invite us up to join him. We cannot take away his freedom of choice. Paul, call out those blocks right now.''

''Unrealism, insecurity, system, image, pride, roles I play, the church, blaming others, resentment, fear . . .''

''Which one is strongest right now, Paul?''

After a pause, ''Resentment and fear, I guess.''

''Finish the sentence as many times as you can, 'I resent . . . ,' and name your resentments and the persons involved.''

With his head still in his hands and his eyes hidden, Paul began. ''I resent the church taking all my time. I resent Mr. Brown who always seems to be putting me down. I resent Mrs. Green who tells stories about me behind my back. I resent my fellow ministers who always seem to have everything going right for them, though I suspect they don't. I resent my wife's pressure (his shoulders began to shake and his voice grew weaker) to come down from this tower and be with her and the family and others more.'' And he sobbed some more.

The house church members were visibly touched by his predicament. His wife's eyes were wet. After he stopped shaking, the leader asked him to voice his feelings again with one change: use the word ''appreciate'' rather than ''resent.''

He began hesitantly, ''I appreciate the church . . . for wanting me.'' That seemed to surprise him. ''I appreciate Mr. Brown for being concerned enough about what I think to dialogue with me. I appreciate my wife's concern—love—for me. She really cares for me. And I shut her out. And I'm still shut up here in my tower, and now I'm afraid to open my eyes. I'm afraid of what people will think. I'm afraid that my wife will reject me when she knows how resentful I've been, how afraid I am, and how I shut myself up in my tower and shut her and the family out.''

''When you are ready, Paul, why don't you try checking out your fears with the members of this church. We love you and care for you, but we are finding it hard to get into that tower with you.''

After a time Paul said, ''I feel so weak, and I've always wanted to appear strong. Right now I am afraid of what all of you will think about this guy who is insecure, weak, fearful, resentful, blaming. That's why I've stayed up in this tower where it is safe—but lonely as hell. I only came down when I could be strong. And now you are asking me to come down when I'm weak. But I'm tired of being alone.'' And with that he jumped, opened his eyes, and looked for his wife. She rushed to meet him with joy coming through her tears. They embraced.

"Is it okay, honey, if I'm not always strong?"

Jane responded with a great sigh of relief. "Of course, you lovely guy. I knew you weren't superman all along, even when I married you. But I can't ever fully love you when you keep hiding up in that tower. You know, I have known about your 'tower,' and sometimes I sneak up there to see what is going on, but you have never invited me in. I hope you will take me with you after this. Whatever is going on with you don't go off alone anymore. That is scary for me.''

They talked some more in the presence of the house church about their relationship. Paul was especially moved by his growing awareness that Jane loved him all the more knowing both his strengths and his weaknesses.

"Paul, there is one more thing which is important for you and for us to do,'' the leader said. "Check out your fear of rejection. Will persons reject you when they find out that you are not as strong as you would like to be? Go around this circle and ask these people. They know about you now.''

Everyone affirmed Paul. Some said that Paul's honest revealing of himself had encouraged them to share their own loneliness, which now they would do. A composite response from the group ran like this: "By letting us know more about you, Paul, you have allowed us to love you more. You seem as human as the rest of us now. We couldn't even reach you in that tower, much less know you and love you. We're glad you've joined the human race. Ministers so often don't.''

It seemed time for a poster which the leader drew from behind a chair and affixed to the wall. It said: Vulnerability Is the Path to Freedom.

Someone began to sing, "Love is something when you give it away you end up having more." Everyone joined in. The singing was not great, but the feeling was honest.

Beth, a young mother participating with her husband, shared her picture next. Her first scene (where she is now) was a sad face in the midst of a group which she told us was her family and friends. Her second scene (where she would like to be) was a happy face in the midst of the same group. Her third drawing (block) was a large question mark. "I don't know what's blocking me," she said. Fourth (what she needs) was a big heart standing for love. As she told us about her picture she expressed her own puzzlement. "I do have a sense of being loved in my family, but I'm often sad, and I don't know why." This was puzzling to the group, too, because they had experienced her ready and contagious laugh on many occasions.

The leader asked her to be the sad face of the first scene, to identify and feel her sadness right now. She closed her eyes. Her face relaxed and drooped. Then she began to cry, softly, unexplainably. "I don't know why these tears keep coming when I've got everything going for me."

"Go behind your eyes and try to find the source of those tears, Beth. Do you see any places or persons?"

Everyone was silent while Beth was looking. Suddenly she began to cry harder. "Yes, my father is there." Lying on her back with her eyes closed, she told us of her mother's death when she was three years old, of her stepmother's goodness, of her father's love for her and of hers for him, of his sudden and unexpected death at the close of her high school career eighteen years ago.

The leader asked, "Can you see your father now?"

"Oh, yes, it's as if he is here right now," Beth replied.

"Talk to your father. Tell him all the things you have wanted to say to him, questions you have wanted to ask him, and listen for his answers. The house church is all around you supporting you in your grief. Keep your eyes closed. I'll hold your hand as our contact with you." She clutched the leader's hand tightly, softly crying. Then quietly she began to speak.

"Dad, I've missed you so much. I keep thinking how nice it would have been if you could have seen me graduate from high school and college . . . how I want you to be grandfather to my three children and you're gone. I've missed you so. Why did you have to go, Dad?" Beth was quiet for a long minute.

"Does he say anything or look any different? Speak for him."

"Why, he's crying too! 'I didn't want to leave you, Beth. I've missed you too. It was very hard for me, and I'm sorry it's been so hard for you.'"

Beth continued to talk with her father. "I had no idea it was hard for you. It just felt like you left, almost without saying good-bye. I was really angry with you, but I could never say that. All the relatives wanted me to be strong, not weak. They wanted me to be a good girl and not angry. But I loved you so, and suddenly you were gone." Beth began crying very loudly, her body shaking. "So I was strong and good. Is it all right, Dad, that I was angry?" There was a long moment filled with sobs which gradually subsided. Then she said to the leader, "He says it's all right. He's sorry he had to go."

"Are you going to say good-bye to him?" the leader asked gently.

"Not yet," Beth replied. "There is something more I must say to him." She tells him about her husband and her children. "You'd love them, Dad."

Her dad replied, "I know I would because you love them. I'd like to bounce them on my knee the way I did you."

"I remember. I remember. It was such fun, and we would laugh and laugh." Beth began to laugh through her tears.

The leader asked, "Is your father laughing too? I imagine you laugh like your father."

"Yes, he is! Dad, I've got your laugh! He says he's glad about that."

"Is there anything else you want to say to him before you say good-bye?" the leader asked.

"Yes, but I'm scared." She paused for a few moments and then resumed her fantasy. "You so much wanted me to be a

concert pianist. And I was good, but I never could be good
enough. My hands just weren't big enough. So I quit in college. I
still play and sing in church and with groups. But I've always
wondered if it was okay with you that I quit.''

Her dad replies, ''Of course it's okay with me. I'm glad you
decided for yourself, that's what I really wanted for you. You
know, I worried about your hands. I guess I knew you would have
trouble.''

Beth gave a great sigh with her whole body. Then she ad-
dressed the leader and the house church, ''I do not want to say
good-bye to Dad. I'll never forget him.''

The leader replied, ''We know that. He's going to live with you
forever in your memory. Although he is physically gone, it feels
as though you've never let him go, never finally accepted his
physical absence.''

Beth was quiet for some moments. ''That's true. It's hard.
Dad, I love you and—(crying)—good-bye. Good-bye, Dad.''

''Does he say anything or do anything?'' the leader asked.

''He says, 'So long, Beth!' And he made a familiar little
gesture with his hand and arm . . . and gave me a beautiful
smile.'' The room was silent. Minutes later, Beth opened her
eyes, smiling through the tears. ''I had no idea all that feeling was
left in me after all these years. I feel great. Like a load has been
lifted from my head, like I don't have to be sad about Dad
anymore. Where's Bill?'' (her husband).

He was right there and moved quickly to her side. She looked at
him as if seeing him in a new way. ''Bill, you look different. It's
as if my sadness has kept my eyes from really seeing you. I want a
big, long hug.'' The house church shouted its approval and, after
a minute, enclosed both Beth and Bill in a bear hug, a big love
ball, the leader called it.

Beth's unfinished grief work with her father triggered work by
several other people in the group who became aware of how they
had been hanging on to loved ones who are gone. Throughout the
day, one experience led to another. We lived through the whole
range of human emotion; we shared memories; we recognized our

own feelings and attitudes and actions in the situations of others. Pain and happiness, tears and laughter, joy and sorrow, despair and hope, love and fear, anger and tenderness were all present.

There were those of us who were still fighting parental control, although the controlling parent frequently lived in a distant part of the country or was deceased. Some were going through the pain of a dissolving marriage, separation and divorce, and wondering what went wrong. Some were troubled over the behavior of their children and blaming themselves. Among us was a man who had just lost his third job in three years, and a woman facing an empty nest with no marketable skills and no work experience, both feeling useless. The whole of the human scene was there—truth stranger and more fascinating than any fiction.

Late Saturday evening Jan shared her picture of her life. The first scene depicted Jan, alone, separated from a group. The second showed her as part of and sharing with the same group. The third was a symbol, a wall separating Jan from the group. Strength, courage, and support were her needs symbolized in the fourth scene. There were few details and little to go on.

We asked questions of information to fill the picture in. Jan was married, her husband John was present. She was pursuing a career in nursing as one of the supervisors on a ward where the staff was predominantly black and Chicano. She was one of the few whites on the ward. Jan had a long history as a member of a church committed to racial equality and justice; she had participated in civil rights marches. But she felt baffled by her present situation and very much alone. Her standards of patient care were often violated by the nurses on her shift. Although she would have called whites on the carpet or opened up discussions in staff sessions, she had stifled her professional supervisory skills because she felt she could not question or criticize the blacks or Chicanos in any way. She was afraid and alone. She had been hiding her professional concerns, her sense of justice, and her own identity. She wanted her staff to become increasingly skilled health care specialists, but she felt blocked from sharing her expertise with them.

Jan knew that she was really blocking herself, but she did not know how she could get over the wall. The leader asked her to identify with the wall in her third picture. "Be the wall. Speak for it. 'I am . . . ' whatever the wall is or feels like to you."

Jan began slowly. "I am a wall. I'm high so no one can see over me. I'm hard and solid. I'm impenetrable. No one can get through me or see through me. If anyone runs into me they get hurt. I show no emotion or color. I'm dull and drab. I'm silent."

There was a long pause as Jan appeared to be thinking very hard. Finally someone said, "Is that the way Jan, the supervisor, is on the job?"

Jan replied, "I had never thought of it that way before, but that's right. I am wall-like on the job. I haven't said much. I don't let anyone see into me. I've probably appeared hard, emotionless, and dull. And that's not really me." The group agreed about that. They had never seen Jan as wall-like. "Furthermore, I'm so frustrated because in a way I'm just where I want to be with a chance to do something about injustice, race relations, upgrading health care, helping minority groups take their rightful place. And I'm acting wall-like."

The leader had a suggestion. "Jan, I'd like to hear you talk to one of the nurses for whom you are responsible. You sit in this chair as Jan, say whatever you like, then move over to this chair and speak for the nurse, whatever you feel she would say."

Remembering the open- and closed-fist experience of the previous evening, Jan had many questions to ask the leader about what to say and why such an exercise had any meaning. He said that he was suggesting a tryout, a way of dealing with her problem in our presence, where we could share how we had experienced her in the conversation. Satisfied, she didn't know how to begin. Someone suggested that she share with the nurse how frustrated she was and how alone and see what happened. Jan agreed.

"Dellinea, I want to talk to you a little about the floor and the staff . . . . I feel . . . I really feel rather . . . separated from you and all the staff. I don't like it, and I don't really want it that way at all. I was wondering how you felt about it?"

Jan moved to the empty chair and spoke for Dellinea. "Well, I'm not surprised, Mrs. Johnson. Some of us have wondered about you. Seems like you just sit at your desk and never come and have coffee with us. Once I thought about asking you, but I guess I was kind of afraid of you."

Jan returned to her own chair. "Afraid of me? Isn't that funny. I've been afraid of you. I would like to have coffee with you."

The nurse replied, "That would be great."

"There's another thing. Sometimes I haven't been too happy with the way some of the nurses talk to the patients or with some of the work which seems sloppy."

"Do you mean me, Mrs. Johnson?"

Jan hesitated, "Well . . . on one thing, yes. The way you . . ." (and she launched into a procedural description of patient care).

Dellinea replied, "You never told me, Mrs. Johnson. I really didn't know any other way. I do wish you had told me earlier. I would appreciate your showing me how."

"I'll do that, Dellinea, first thing tomorrow morning." She paused and then continued. "One other thing, Dellinea, which I'm embarrassed to ask. Is it all right with you that I'm white and your supervisor?"

Dellinea replied frankly. "Well, it's okay. I would like to see a black supervisor on this floor sometime. Mostly, it would be more fun if you were—more human. Let yourself go. Be one of us. Be supervisor, just be fair, and let us know where we stand. I kind of like you now after this talk."

Jan stopped her dialogue and turned to the group. "I have no idea if that is the way it would go, but there are certainly a lot of things I can do to change how I have been on that floor. I don't feel so scared now about engaging in conversation with Dellinea."

The house church members contributed their perceptions of how they had experienced the dialogue, and they encouraged Jan. They negotiated a contract with her about what she would do on the job before the group met again in two weeks. After some discussion, Jan agreed to talk with two nurses, join the group for coffee, and consciously be Jan and not a wall. The last item of the contract was nebulous, but Jan said she had a very good idea of how that might be. Someone suggested she try it out right now in the house church by going around the group, first being wall-like with each member and then switching to being Jan-like. She took to this suggestion with alacrity and zest. Hilarity and fun ensued. Jan reported how strongly she had felt her power to switch back and forth and how much better being Jan-like felt.

As Saturday evening ended, almost every one of the sixteen who had gathered together Friday evening had worked through some of the knots and hang-ups of his own life and listened and responded to the hurts and confusions of the others. Although no sure cures or certain salvation had been promised, the group's summation showed that two headaches had left, two backaches had greatly diminished, several marriages had found new starting places, and many contracts had been made to change behavior on the job or at home. The group agreed to report to one another at their next meeting and to call upon one another for help or support in between times if necessary.

A climate of affirmation and love enveloped us all. Sally said, "I'm amazed that you care; I didn't think anyone did other than my family. Is this what the church is all about?"

Tom volunteered, "Before I came here I thought I had friends. Now I know what a friend really is."

Although not everyone had shared a picture, everyone felt quite secure and cared for by the group. No one had been attacked or pooh-poohed or rejected, no matter what secrets were revealed, what hurt and pain was relived, what anxiety was confronted. Everyone's life had had joy and sorrow. The miracle was that sharing the sorrow increased the joy. We had wept with and for one another and had laughed and sung and danced, and we were tired. So we went to bed.

We spent Sunday morning, from breakfast to lunch, doing feedback. What an experience! Each of us, in turn, listened to the group tell us what and how they felt about us in three categories: Get, Give, and Flush. We took it down on large sheets of paper.

Get is the category of those qualities, skills, or behaviors which some member of the group would like to get from us; *Give* refers to gifts the house church members would like to give to us; *Flush* is a listing of our behaviors and attitudes which the house church members felt were so handicapping they would like us to get rid of them. The feedback experience was affirming. Rarely does one hear from even one other which behaviors or attitudes seem helpful and which ones are counterproductive. To have a whole roomful of people give careful and loving attention to one another is a new experience. One need no longer guess or imagine how one's behavior is being seen and felt by others.

Jan's feedback sheet, which she folded and took home—as we all did—looked like this:

Get   smile   sense of justice
       sensitivity to persons and to pain
       care about others   easy relation to husband
       awareness of the body
       soft touch
       expression of warmth when relaxed

Give   courage to risk   hammer to break wall
        freedom to be Jan in all situations
        support   awareness of her strength
        money for the coffee breaks
        power to ''see'' her nurses in a new way
        spontaneity with emotions

Flush   the wall
         fear of what others will think
         worry
         desk you sit behind
         mask
         hardness at work

After Sunday lunch we spent about thirty minutes reflecting—''doing theology''—about our house church experience. How, or in what ways, was our experience together Christian? How can the experiences of this weekend be understood in the light of the biblical story, the history of the church? We wrote and wrote; ideas and images came easily; we didn't have enough time.

In the center of our circle the leader had placed a loaf of bread and a jug of wine. We created our own ways of eating and drinking, of sharing communion with one another. Some people read the reflections which they had just written. Some shared their thoughts about the meaning of the symbols and the sacraments, of both this particular house church and the larger church which many of us were part of. Others reflected on new meanings which they had found in familiar biblical phrases and stories.

The image of the casting out of demons came to me in this house church. Some demons were looked full in the face, seen as poor shadowy things having no real power but kept alive by an incapacitating memory. They were done in completely.

Some were so beaten as to be seriously weakened, their grasp enfeebled. But more there are, in each of us, expanding to fill the void, which they will do unless a new power or love or sense of wholeness rushes in.

*   *   *   *   *

This weekend the Word became flesh and dwelt among us. The words, "If you cannot love your neighbor whom you have seen, how can you love God whom you have not seen?" took on new meaning for me.

*   *   *   *   *

"Where two or three are gathered together in my name, there am I in the midst of them." I felt that the promise of the Christ was at least partially fulfilled in our time together.

*   *   *   *   *

I saw my own life story in relation to the liberation story told by the Bible—Abraham going out, Moses and Israel moving out of Egypt, Jesus setting people free from narrowness and sin. I come out of this experience with a feeling that I have found a new freedom and can, therefore, tell Good News about the love that is available to us all.

*   *   *   *   *

Yesterday I experienced the resurrection. My friends literally transported me through death so that I could experience rebirth. God! How hard it is to accept that people do love you! What a wonderful experience to know that they love you, care deeply about you, and will not let you go. I have been floating ever since. How I suffered. . . . Maybe this is the greatest manifestation of God's love I shall ever know.

We sang, we prayed, we danced, we hugged one another, and we went home with our feedback sheets folded under our arms. We were new persons, with new understandings and insights and behaviors, eager to try ourselves out in the outside world. We would be off our cultural island, but we were secure in the knowledge that it exists. We know that there are people close at hand who know us, accept us, and love us without conditions, with no strings attached.

Grace.

Joy.

Freedom.

2. House Church Theory

At the base of all human behavior, both individual and institutional, is a belief, a set of values, a basic premise. Often it is unspoken, unwritten, even unclear. It sometimes takes a lot of questioning and thought to uncover it, but it is there.

What is the basis of the church's activities, week in, week out? Often they are unexamined. In many cases what the church professes to *believe* and what it *does* are opposed. A great expenditure of the time and energy of both clergy and laity is often used in keeping the machinery of the organization going, the meetings scheduled, the calendar straight, the money raised. Only now and then does a person have an experience in the church of unremitting, unconditional love. Everyone needs to be loved, clergy as well as laity; everyone wants to be loved. The church is an institution built on love. Yet only a few people experience, in the church, love which will not let them go. Our hymns and prayers and litanies are full of it. We are taught that God loves us, but we experience it infrequently.

Love is what the house church is all about; love made real in the lives of men and women; love not only verbalized but also actualized; love incarnate, made flesh, an authentic part of human relationships.

God's love made operational in the lives of persons is the Good News, the reason for churches and for all activities churches support. The house church is one way in which the Good News can be experienced. It is not the only way, either within the church or without. The house church movement borrows whatever skills and insights from contemporary education, sociology, psychology, anthropology, and the human potential movement may serve its purpose, whatever will enable persons to work and love more freely and sensitively, less defensively, secretively, tensely.

To love a person wholly is to commit oneself to that person's well-being, to listen, to respond, to be present. House church members do this for one another and quickly develop bonds of caring and concern. Having ears, we hear; having eyes, we see; being human, we know how it feels. One of our Roman Catholic friends calls the house church the meat and potatoes of the total church, the substantive center which provides the nourishment for all the rest of it.

It is the commitment of house church members to love and care for one another in God's name which sets the house church apart from small group experiences outside the church. Neither sensitivity groups, nor encounter groups, nor therapy groups are founded on the premise which is basic to the house church: love incarnate is the Good News which is available to all women and men. Nor does any other small group seek the same goal as the house church: to experience the Good News and enable others to experience it as well.

There are many crises in a lifetime, problems which are personal, cultural, philosophical, even doctrinal. Persons are mobile and uprooted, finding limited opportunities to belong; anxious, discovering that yesterday's answer does not fit today's problem, and yesterday's moral behaviors are considered irrelevant and unnecessary; separated, speaking a language and jargon peculiar to their own field, thus experiencing difficulty in carrying on meaningful communication with persons in other fields; fearful, being in a job which prizes competition over cooperation; lonely, living—often alone—through old age, separation and divorce, widowhood, the "empty nest" stage; useless, finding either that one's skills, education, and experience cannot provide one with something to do or to be in society, or that a lifetime of experience is of little value to the young and can be easily and lightly discarded; guilty, knowing that relationships at home or at work are going sour rather than growing strong; grieving, feeling hurt and anger and guilt over the death of a loved one, maybe even years ago. Two incomes per family or being young or being established or being retired do not dispel all these problems. Meaninglessness, hopelessness, hurt, pain, and anger do not go away with affluence or age. The context changes, the circumstances are different, but the feelings remain the same.

Psychological and Theological Understandings of Man

There are two definable aspects of house church process —communal and individual. Each aspect affects, contributes to, empowers the other. Together they make a whole.

Christianity is both individual and communal. "You shall love the Lord your God . . . and your neighbor as yourself" (Luke 10:27). There is a priority: self-love precedes other love. As our son says it, "A person has to get his own act together before he can do anything that counts." When we become able to handle hurt or anger or grief, when we are enabled to accept ourselves, to love ourselves, to own our feelings, then we are increasingly able to love God and be related to the people about us. As we change, our relationships to others change. Conversely, the more people about us change in the ways in which they relate to us the more we change in our relationships to them. Like the chicken and the egg, it's not easy to be sure which came first, but the fact that each has an effect on the other is indisputable.

The goal of the house church is to become a loving, trusting community within which persons can change, become whole, be enabled to love, to feel of worth, and to take charge of their own lives.

A whole person is a unity, a body with a mind and a heart, an entity of thoughts, feelings, and actions which are interrelated and which affect one another. At a particular time, any one of these three parts may predominate, but none of them is independent of the other two. For example, at one time I think about the shoplifting problems of the department stores and the supermarkets (thinking); at another time, I become angry that I have to pay for someone else's thievery through higher prices (feeling); at still another time, I talk with the store manager about the merchandising and pricing policies which have resulted from shoplifting (acting). Obviously, talking with the manager (acting) involves thinking and feeling about shoplifting. Even when there is no acting, thinking and feeling always go together.

When thinking and feeling and acting are functioning together, when none of them is suppressing, ignoring, or distorting some of

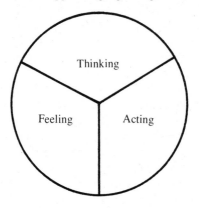

Figure 1. A Whole Person

the data which the person confronts, the person experiences congruency, wholeness. He is experiencing himself fully, objectively, realistically.

The aspect of the whole person which most often is ignored is the *feeling* part. Anger, in many Christian circles, is not acceptable. It must not be expressed straightforwardly, and it must not be acted out. "You don't fight in church," we have heard Sunday school teachers say. Most adults would agree. So if a person feels anger or grief or fear and learns not to express it on pain of disapproval, he eventually denies the feeling even to himself. A feeling denied, however, is never done in; it is only put down. It becomes well covered, protected. It lies deep, out of sight and unrecognizable to most people, including the person himself. Even he does not know it is there.

Each of us has learned in our growing up that these three parts—thinking, feeling, acting—stand in a hierarchy of importance. No one came out and said it, but we learned it nevertheless. Thinking is most important; that's what schooling is all about. Acting is second; that's what living in the world is all about. Feeling is third, least important. The only times anyone must be concerned with feelings, his own or others', is when they get in the way of thinking and acting.

All this is not true, of course, in spite of the fact that most churches and schools and families carry out their activities in terms of these assumptions. Accordingly, children grow up believing that they know something if they can think it, organize it, relate it, analyze it, verbalize it. They learn that to feel or to act is not required in order to know.

This assumption is not altogether true either. One can know algebraic formulae on a solely intellectual level, but love and trust and forgiveness cannot be known completely by the mind alone. One must feel loved and give and take love in order to know what love is. Similarly, to know what trust is, or forgiveness, or reconciliation, or acceptance, or grace, or any of the eternal truths which hold life together and which help people maintain both loving and accepting attitudes toward themselves and honest, open, loving relationships with one another, one must experience them fully. One must think them, feel them, act them.

A whole person has three dimensions, and each dimension has three levels, as figure 2 shows. The levels differ from one another in terms of the time and distance from the present which characterize each of them. To be specific: level one includes the long ago and far away, the objective, the theoretical, the imper-

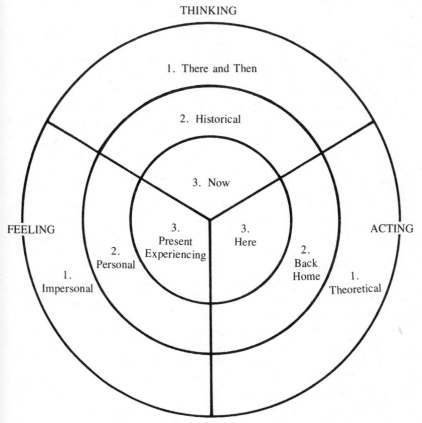

Figure 2. Levels and Dimensions of the Whole Person

sonal, the there and then; level two includes the long ago but not so far away, the subjective, the personal; level three is right now and right here, the "present experiencing." There is interplay between dimensions and levels. The house church focuses on level three at the center, the here and now, the present experiencing of thoughts, feelings, actions.

There are many ways to talk about, think about, diagram a whole person. Every field of thought has its own models and spokespersons. Most of them agree that our society has emphasized the development of the intellect, with some experiencing of levels one and two to the neglect of the psyche and the experiencing of level three. We have inherited and accepted without careful examination a view of the person as having two parts, a mind and a body which can function independently of each other, and a view of the present as less important than the future. Our language reveals these points of view: "put your mind to it," "mind over matter," "save it for a rainy day." The facts are that a large percentage of persons who are fired from their jobs are failures in human relationships, not in intellectual competence; many of those who occupy hospital beds have a distress of the psyche which is the source of the dis-ease of the body; the rainy day never comes. A two-part person with a future orientation does not feel or understand or appreciate the problems or the joys of the present moment.

Wholeness and its opposite condition, fragmentation or brokenness, have long been the concern of the Christian church. We are called to love one another and ourselves. Self-giving love has been our model and is our typifying characteristic in a loveless, greedy world. "See how these Christians love one another," Tertullian, the early churchman wrote in the second century. We often fail; we are not able to love one another unremittingly and unconditionally, and we cannot altogether love ourselves, for we know about our unlovely parts which we keep hidden. The commandment to love God, neighbor, and self requires wholeness as a precondition. The translator of Matthew who wrote "You, therefore, must be perfect" (5:48) could also have written "You therefore must be whole,'' for the original Greek word carries both meanings.

There are three anchor points, or theological concepts, which undergird the house church. These concepts are operational ones; that is, everything that is said or done in the house church meetings illustrates or has reference to one or another of these related ideas. A fragmented person has experienced failures in love, in worth, or in keeping covenants.

Love. It is paradoxical that when a person is most in need of love, he is least likely to do what is necessary to get it. From an early age on, we do not behave so that we get what we want. Parents and teachers know that when a child needs love most is when he is most unlovable. We frustrate ourselves, distance ourselves, do not ask for what we need, imagine that others know what we need without our telling them. Consequently, we often feel unloved and are convinced that we are unlovable. Love is a primary need of every human being; it is the glue of the house church. "Greater love has no man than this, that a man lay down his life for his friends" (John 15:13). To lay down one's life for another is to die for him. Few of us are called to do that. All of us are called to live for one another, to hear, to see, to feel, to care for another without growing weary. Such loving is hard to do.

Worth. Every person needs not only to love and to be loved, but also to be considered a person of worth. I need to be valued for myself, not for my sex, my looks, my skills, my education, my job, my attitudes. I am *somebody*. I need to believe that about myself and I need you to believe it about me.

So are you *somebody*. You are my brother or sister. In God's eyes there are no conditions of worth, no greater or lesser intrinsic value between male and female, black and white, executive and worker, Chinese, Russian, and American. "There is neither Jew nor Greek, there is neither slave nor free, there is neither male nor female; for you are all one in Christ Jesus" (Gal. 3:28).

Infusing a people with a sense of worth, a personal transformation which will culminate in social transformation, is one of the goals of Operation PUSH. The four thousand participants at the Saturday morning meetings of PUSH (formerly Operation Bread-basket) in Chicago affirm their worth and the significance of the black experience and black power by proclaiming "I am *somebody*. We are *somebody*." When we realize our intrinsic worth, our whole outlook toward ourselves, toward others, to-ward God changes.

Covenants. A third area of distress in the life of a fragmented person frequently concerns promises and responsibilities to sig-nificant others. Secrets which involve experiences of broken con-tracts are sources of disquiet. Even if the world does not know, the keeper of the secret knows and is often fearful, lonely, alienated. He is out of communication. He lives with great anxi-ety about the past (guilt), about the present (meaninglessness, frustration), and about the future (insecurity, hopelessness).

Each of us lives with a number of covenants: a marriage covenant, a work covenant, a family covenant, a citizen cove-nant. When we act irresponsibly and do not keep a covenant or fulfill a covenant, we experience estrangement and distrust. The Judeo-Christian history relates similar experiences with an entire people. When the Hebrews kept their covenant with God, they knew peace, harmony, good will. When they broke their cove-nant, they suffered countless troubles. Covenants can be re-negotiated, but not by one party alone, in secret.

The church believes that we can learn to love ourselves, our neighbor, and God; that we are created in God's image and are of great worth, to be valued; that a broken covenant between persons or between a person and God will result in disquiet and dishar-mony, even as a kept covenant results in well-being and peace. The house church seeks to give these truths reality by enabling persons to experience them with one another.

How does a person feel when fragmented? How does a person think and feel and act when whole? What will help a person move from fragmentation to wholeness? The house church, in the tradi-tion of the Christian church from its first-century beginnings, is a response to these age-old, still-with-us questions.

How does a person think and feel and act when fragmented? A fragmented person thinks and feels unloved and worthless, troubled, grieved, unfulfilled, guilty, unfree, angry, or afraid. When I am fragmented, I am ambivalent, confused, depressed, energyless. I feel that I am a lost sheep whom no one is seeking, sinful, imperfect, inadequate. I use much of my psychic energy to hold myself together, to keep my problems and my anxieties under control. Sometimes I feel like a man on a horse riding off in six directions, or a beetle stuck on a pin, or a swimmer dog-paddling in the treacherous sea. Fragmented persons may be carrying secrets that need to be shared, or they may have broken some covenants which they promised to keep and they feel alienated, separated, estranged.

How does a person think and feel and act when whole? Of course it is not true that there are no fragmentations or problems or vexations in wholeness. Everyone has something that needs to be worked on. But when one's predominant sense of self is wholeness rather than fragmentation, one radiates a sense of well-being in all one's relationships. "God's in his heaven—All's right with the world." When I am feeling most whole, I love people and they love me. I do not feel alone or lonely; I belong to someone. Because I can contribute to the life of those about me, I feel of worth. I am somebody, related to all the world's somebodies, concerned for them and responsible to them. Whole persons are authentic, open, honest, trusting and trustworthy. They keep their covenants.

What will help a person move from fragmentation to wholeness? Sharing one's doubts, hopes, pain, secrets; confessing one's errors, poor judgments, hurtful behaviors; expressing one's confusions, ambivalences, anger; discovering that one has been heard, understood, and cared for by a group of persons who seek only the fragmented person's wholeness. The everlasting arms which are underneath are the arms of one's friends. They support, they uphold, they are there, without question or condition.

The process of moving from fragmentation to wholeness is

twofold, requiring both individual and communal action. The fragmented person must disclose himself, and the members of the house church must receive the disclosure with love. If either half of this process does not take place, growth toward wholeness for any one person is incomplete, and growth toward becoming a piece of the caring Christian community (which the house church strives to be) develops slowly and with difficulty.

Throughout its history the church has returned again and again to some kind of form in which face-to-face groups of Christians meet to minister to one another. The house church stands in a long line of small groups where Christians have sought to be transformed, or to be healed, or to find a new and more fulfilling orientation for their lives. The earliest Christian church described in the New Testament met in the homes of its members, for the synagogues which housed the religious establishment of that day were not available to this new movement. Paul writes in I Corinthians 16:19, "Aquila and Prisca, together with the church in their house, send you hearty greetings in the Lord."

The Methodist Church began in the eighteenth century in cottage meetings in the homes of members; the established Church of England was not available to them. The evangelical revivals of the nineteenth century in Sweden found meeting places in homes because the Lutheran State Church was not open to them. Many Amish people in the United States today meet regularly for church in one another's farmhouses. Houses as meeting places have served committed Christians from the church's beginning.

Even the architecture of the earliest church buildings is evidence of the house beginnings of the church. Churches were enlarged homes, with the same central features of an ante room and a larger living room. The loving fellowship of persons became the *ecclesia* of the New Testament. Later the church as an institution developed to protect and formalize the *ecclesia*'s experiencing of the life of love in Christ. The first generation wanted to guarantee the experience of love and care for the children and grandchildren. But institutionalizing the experience of love cannot be done. It becomes easier to maintain the forms than to enter into the experience. A new generation finds the forms restrictive and seeks again the authentic experience which the forms seek to ensure. The institutional form for the experience of love, which was authentic for previous generations, has become wooden and binding and inhibiting, even irrelevant, to many Christians in the twentieth century.

The generation gap is always with us. Because we want to save good things, we often make the mistake of trying to *structure the forms* of an experience instead of *enabling the process* which made the experience possible. Man is idolatrous by nature. He creates idols out of the form under which he experiences love. Summer youth conferences are an illustration. Not long ago persons experienced the love which is the base of the church in this setting. Conferences and camps were institutionalized; they became a large and important part of the program designed by every major denomination. Today's generation finds little meaning, insight, or relevance in camps and conferences. There's nothing wrong with the campground; the *form* is all right. The deficiency is with the program; the *process,* the living, the experiencing is often dull, contrived, unimportant. Today church camps go begging for participants.

It is altogether possible that the house church may become identified as a particular form rather than as a process. Wherever and whenever that happens, its death is certain. Like all forms, it will become wooden, rigid, sterile. It is house church process which is here described and affirmed.

Here is a reflection sheet filled out at the close of an intensive weekend house church along with a letter which came later. Together they emphasize the love and worth and increased covenantal responsibility experienced by the participant.

1. What were your feelings and expectations, prior to the start of this house church?

I had no idea what to expect. I had heard a variety of things about sensitivity groups and didn't know what this one would be like, but it was something I wanted very much to do. I felt a real need to touch more lives intimately. The past year I had learned the meaning of the word "friend." Perhaps this would be a way of giving back some of what had been given to me and at the same time gain more for myself and for others. Only in the last couple of months have I felt "ready" for such an experience, for I have only recently begun to find a real wholeness and integration after the shattering experience of my divorce.

2. What did you experience during the house church? (As to feelings, ideas, bodily action, etc.)

How can it be said on a piece of paper? It will take a lifetime of living to say it.

When some of our church members came home from a house church conference and talked of the sharing of Christian love and concern with hugs, etc., I stoutly maintained they weren't necessary. It was an "attitude," I said; a simple handclasp, a smile, a pat on the back would do the same. Now I know.

I am very much encouraged that the Christian church is finding this vitality, this method of ministering to the basic need of people.

For me personally the great thing was that I *cried*.

> Two years I talked
> Impersonally
> As if from a great distance
> Tremendous depth of feeling inside
> But the dam held
> My voice was calm, controlled.
> I fought it;
> I withdrew from the group;
> I was forced back;
> Knowing the concern that would be felt about my absence;
> But I had repaired the dam.
> It held.
> But when I least expected it, it broke;
> Great, gushing sobs broke forth.
> As the water rushed out
> Love came flooding in
> And with it
> Peace.

I suspect this was the experience of many—and it welded us into a church.

3. How did your perceptions of other people (significant others, present or not present in the house church) alter?

The two who came with me knew the facts about me, but I had not let them glimpse the inner core of my real suffering, nor had I been permitted to see the depth of suffering that Erica has endured these many years. How different it is now! But you ask *how* has this changed as if you expect ordinary people using ordinary words to express, *explain* this. How!!???

But some of it can be hinted at, pointed to. I became much more acutely aware that underneath the masks we all wear is a great reservoir of fears, joys, angers, frustrations, and we're every one afraid to lift the mask and let others see inside. Maybe we would say we let God see, but just an ethereal God, not the God who is present in others. Oh, yes, I would have said I knew it before. But I knew it only with my head. Now I know with my heart, and I shall be looking for cracks in the armor of others, not that I may probe, but that I may share, for I know that a real sharing brings release. I'm afraid that in the past I've missed many clues, been unaware of many cries for help. I'll miss some in the future, but I'll respond more readily.

4. What potential do you see in this process? (Respond as you wish to some or all of the following.)
—for re-forming your vision of the church?
—for enriching or changing your theological understanding?
—for forming styles of ministry?
—for relating personal encounter with institutional and social change?
—for learning in theological education?
—for training for ministry?

Here in this room is the church—not a building or a social club—the *church*. For as many years as I can remember I've known something was wrong with what we glibly call the church. But I didn't even know how to make a beginning toward righting that wrong. Here, if not *the* way, is *a* way. The past year I've agonized, struggled, prayed, read, and have finally formulated a neat little theology that I like. This could disturb it—but I won't let it—not yet—not yet—but no, I have to have a system that satisfies both mind and heart.

Man! The implications for changing styles of ministry and training for the ministry are tremendous. I definitely think this should be a big part of training for ministers.

May 29

Dear Fred

(Just to orient you—I'm the divorcee with the "no one will be able to see me as a worthwhile human being" problem.)

I must share with you some of the follow-up that resulted from last week. On the way home I suddenly realized I must see my former husband. I wanted to do it for him and for myself. I wanted him to know of the integration, wholeness, and joy that I have found—and to relieve him of the guilt I know he has been feeling. For myself I felt this would help me rid myself of him as a husband and begin to relate to him as just another human being. And I think it accomplished both things. He was genuinely relieved, said, "I'm so glad you called me over. This has really been bothering me." My heart ached for him at times—when he said, "I have my belly full of living alone, but things aren't going well with my new wife and me" or "I've withdrawn this year. You've gotten out and done things (crisis volunteer, Great Books, etc.), but I just go home and watch TV."

Formerly I had been afraid even to hear his voice on the telephone. The other night I hugged him before he left and said "Good-bye as a husband. Hello as a human being."

I had never thought of myself as a strong person; but you said it with such conviction that I began to believe it too—and so I am. Thank you!

Have your wife or daughter give you a hug for me.

                                    Love,

Let me share with you, also, the poem that resulted from my weekend experiences.

> The synthesis!
> At last the synthesis!
> The thesis and the antithesis
> How well have I known them.
> Love and hate
> Joy and sorrow
> Pleasure and pain
> Rejoicing and grief
> Laughter and tears—
> Now—through grace—shall they all become *One*
> I shall know deep contentment
> Mixed with a depth of suffering.
> And guilt shall blend with forgiveness.
> Loneliness shall know togetherness.
> Peace shall quiet turmoil.
> Failure shall be clothed with success.
> Ignorance shall be blessed with understanding.
> "And the earth shall be full of the knowledge of the Lord"
> And peace shall reign.

Part 2
The House Church Process

3. Building a Faith-Trust Community

Trust is the root of both personal growth and of relationships with
other persons. In all human relationships—husband-wife,
teacher-pupil, parent-child, friend-friend—the presence of trust
facilitates everything else. Persons who do not grow in their trust
of one another remain isolated and alone.

No one can be entirely self-sufficient; a minimal level of trust is
built into the social order. As we write these words we are trusting
a host of people to provide warmth, light, food, and innumerable
physical supports for our lives. The street repair and street cleaning crews make automobile transportation possible for us. Air-
plane mechanics make it possible for us to work with church
persons half a continent away while maintaining a teaching relationship with students within three blocks of us. The garbage
pickup crews keep the food input-output system operating. Elec-
tric light maintenance sets the street lights to come on and off

outside our doors as the hours of daylight change throughout the year.The dairy men and women in farm and factory prepare the milk which comes dependably clean and pure to our table. The newsmen and newswomen keep us informed about what's going on all over the world via press, radio, and television. We trust people to provide for us; in fact, we need people to provide for us. If they did not, we would die.

But, we are not only physical beings. We are also persons with emotions, hopes, despairs, joys, and sorrows. Physical support is not enough. We need emotional support. We want to belong to others, to relate to others, to be affirmed by others. We will die as persons if we do not trust others to care for our emotions as we trust them to care for our bodies.

Trust is putting one's life in the hands of another person or persons. We hunger for relationships where we can disclose who we are or who we have been and be accepted. However, persons can only accept us if we trust them with something of our lives which needs to be accepted. No one can accept the real us if we have trusted him or her with nothing important to us or with a mask or a phony story.

Persons will accept the bits and pieces, the insignificant items, if that is what we disclose. But we will continue to feel alone and isolated because we know that there is important further truth about ourselves. Would the other person accept all that? To get the love we seek, we must disclose everything that is important to us. Only then can we be fully accepted. If we still feel unaccepted or unacceptable, the chances are that there is still a part of us which we have not entrusted to others.

No one can be forced to trust. To trust others with all one's life is a choice each person makes in each relationship. There are things one doesn't do and things one does do. One does not give up one's identity, submit to others' wishes, persuade or conceal in order to avoid disapproval, falsify oneself for the sake of phony peace and harmony. A person strives to be himself openly, freely. In a relationship of trust there is mutuality. As each person becomes increasingly transparent about his thoughts, his feelings, and his actions, he discovers he is ever more deeply loved and affirmed. Thus trust grows. Hand in hand with love. Which comes first is a "chicken or the egg" question.

There is no doubt of the necessity for experiencing love and trust in infancy from the first hours of life. Indeed, a child not experiencing trust as an infant will find it hard to be a trusting adult. But trust is not accomplished once and for all at any point in life. It needs to be reexperienced again and again, at different times and places, with different people. To give and to receive trust is an ongoing need of each person.

A faith-trust community of love (which a house church is) ought to be, on the face of it, the most natural, necessary, and easy group to relate to. But it is not. Trusting proves to be very difficult to do. We long to belong, yet we hesitate to trust. We are often afraid, suspicious, cautious, safety conscious, hesitant, waiting for the other person to prove himself trustworthy. The dilemma of trust was well put by a member of a house church who wrote:

> I find it very difficult to trust people, both from lack of experience and opportunity, and I must know them before I will do so. I was afraid, because of the nature of the house church, that I would be forced to trust a group of people I was uneasy with because I did not know them. (The question of how one comes to know someone did not occur to me.) In addition, I was afraid if I did trust them to the point that I would talk, that what I revealed would not be acceptable to others. One who has been and is lonely and has not learned to live with that must protect himself by being as acceptable as possible. I was a combination of skepticism, fear, and hope that nothing would happen or that something would happen.

The Development of Trust

We want and need to belong. But we hesitate to trust. Why? Because our behavior has been disapproved of, or we've been belittled or shamed, or our trust has been betrayed sometime along the way.

Each person begins life completely dependent upon other persons for life itself. The newborn baby cannot survive without the twenty-four-hour care of others, primarily its mother. In the beginning, the total life of the baby is known to the persons who care for it.

As the child grows, there comes a time when the persons who care for it, usually the members of the family, do not know all that is happening to the child. Of what they do know, they either approve or disapprove. The child learns quickly to reveal only those thoughts, feelings, and behaviors which bring approval and to hide those things which bring disapproval.

The teen-age years bring an increasing number of experiences which become part of each child's private world. Choosing persons with whom to share the important feelings, questions, and events of the child's life is one of the steps of growth. In adolescence the young person has many secrets which he keeps from his family. In maturity the growing person chooses new persons with whom he shares his secrets. He trusts a spouse, a friend, a neighbor, a colleague.

Every person wants to trust and to be in communion with others. Sadly, every person also has a personal history of disapproval of behavior or betrayal of trust. Experiences at home, in school, in church, or in the community have often been so destructive and painful that he has retreated to a private, hidden life, unable to secure what he most wants: to belong to others.

Sexuality provides a common example of this growth-of-mistrust process in our lives. The growing child discovers his genitals and the pleasure of fondling his body. In a variety of ways some members of the family may express their disapproval. The child quickly learns to enjoy his body in private and not to trust anybody with this aspect of his life. Reinforced by the schizophrenic sexual attitudes of our society which advertise sexuality everywhere yet disapprove of actual sexual and bodily pleasure, the child becomes adolescent and then adult, unable to trust anyone with his sexual life. Even within marriage, partners are often isolated and alone, unsure and untrusting.

The church, in spite of what it intends, does not promote trust.

Persons come to the church hoping to be known and to be accepted as uniquely able, worthwhile, lovable people, hungering to belong to a community they can trust. They are usually offered a private, individualized salvation. Sunday morning worship, which they attend, sitting in hard, straight-backed pews, looking at the back of someone's head, is deadly liturgical and formalistic. Confession is rarely specific and personal; it is usually general and corporate. Belonging to a face-to-face, ongoing group of persons within the church happens for only a few. Rather than growth in trust, the church goes along with the gold rush syndrome.

In the gold rush days, when a run for a new field was on, a potential prospector didn't dare stop to help another man who was having trouble. If he stopped, he lost time, and someone else, maybe even the man he stopped to help, would beat him out for the best claim. The result was a highly individualized, secretive, private existence. Trusting your neighbor with any information about yourself or about what you knew meant that you might not win. Too many Americans and church people still live that way. We are fearful that disclosing anything about ourselves to a neighbor may be blown out of proportion and used against us in deliberate debasement.

Cooperation is much more of a necessity for our full existence than competition. We know this. We cooperate in churches. We cooperate in huge industrial combines. We cooperate in government and services. But we tend to ignore this knowledge, continuing to talk and feel and act as if we were still on a gold rush. We do not talk to anyone about what really concerns us. We become so adept at deviousness, deceit, half-truths that we lose touch with truth. We deny our feelings so often and so well that we come to believe that they do not exist. When a child's honest expression of hurt or anger is disapproved, he eventually comes to believe that he doesn't have such feelings. Secrecy and emotional dishonesty become characteristic of his style of life. Although he may not know it, he is afraid to be known by others and is unable to engage in give-and-take with them.

Growing a Trusting Community

Immediate present experiencing is the fundamental method of the house church process. What we do is to provide conditions in which the group members can experience trust in the immediate situation. We cannot force anyone to trust. We face the trust issue squarely, accepting everyone's experiencing, and in the process we discover that the trust level is growing. Lectures or sermons about trust, interpretations, theories, references to past groups, theological exhortation, biblical words, psychological inputs we have found to be secondary and almost useless as ways of growing trust in the house church. Many people know all that already. The issue is: Will we trust one another?

There are factors which promote the growth of trust, some very obvious and common, others not so ordinary nor so well known.

The setting. Where a house church meets, for how long, who comes, how many come, and the ground rules of how persons relate to one another are all matters which can promote or impede the growth of trust.

The meeting place should be neutral ground, informal, a place apart, away from phones, doorbells, curious onlookers, and interruptions. It could be a camp or conference ground, a home in the country, or even someone's basement recreation room. Wherever the house church is held must be a private place, where kitchen help and casual traffic will not see or hear or interrupt what is going on. And it should have no intruding clock.

The house church, coming together for the first time, needs to meet long enough to establish itself as a community. Certainly time is required to move the group from the trust-building exercises through the work of personal change to theologizing, celebrating, and communion. From early Friday evening to late Sunday afternoon has been found satisfactory by some churches, with Saturdays beginning early and ending late. Five hours are needed to get acquainted and to engage in trust-building exercises, and at least three hours need to be scheduled for theologizing, celebrating, and communion at the end. If the house church is to be ongoing, additional time must be allowed for preliminary contract building (see chapter 8).

No more than eighteen people should be in a weekend house church. If the house church is scheduled to meet over four or five days, twenty-two people might be in it. These numbers are upper limits; they are determined by the nature of the house church experience. It is almost impossible for more than eighteen persons to relate meaningfully to one another in a weekend. Thirty-one working hours together is just barely enough time for eighteen persons to see, hear, respond to one another. Twelve to fourteen persons is optimum. Nine persons is minimum.

Persons invited to become members of a house church might come from a region, state, conference, or single church. Each situation has its particular opportunities and handicaps in building trust. Since people often stereotype one another according to job and educational level, it has been found helpful for people to introduce themselves to the group by their first names, eliminating all information which assigns status or prestige.

Mealtimes are important in the house church. They provide opportunities for smaller conversations which are often later shared with the entire group. There is usually much fun and good spirit at meals. If there can be something special to eat, so much the better. Homemade bread or ice cream, organic salads, or health foods of many kinds are fun to eat and add to the specialness of the experience.

The ground rules described in chapter 1 are essential; the *don'ts* and *dos* are very valuable in helping persons respond to one another. With the rules posted, one needs only match what one is about to say with the rules, should one have any questions. A person who feels that he can speak or act ''appropriately'' is relaxed about what he says or does and is able to trust and to feel trusted.

Undoubtedly the most critical rule of all is the one which deals with confidentiality. Each person tells his own story; no person tells another's story. Too many hurts occur in our church communities because someone tells another's story, or a version of it. Trust will not grow if persons are afraid of gossip and slander. To reduce anxieties which might stem from such fears, straightforward discussions about confidentiality have to take place in the early part of the house church meeting.

The leadership. We are often asked if a house church has to have a leader. In most cases, yes. There needs to be someone with each group who has particular listening and responding skills. Often this person is a member of the clergy with some training and experience in group work and considerable knowledge of personality. The clergy's education and ordination provide a strong background for learning about leadership of a house church. So does the education and experience of many Christian lay men and women.

The style of the leader greatly affects the development of trust. Our experiences with many house churches have strengthened our convictions about the modeling done by the leader. When we have trusted the group with how we are feeling "right now"—frightened, hopeful, anxious, joyous, fearful, exhilarated—the members have trusted us with how they feel "right now." When we have revealed to the group the fact that our stomach muscles are tense, the members have begun to get in touch with their own bodies and share their feelings. When we have trusted the group with our own struggles in relationship to parents, spouses, children, students, authorities—the painful, the humorous, the hurtful, the rewarding—the members have trusted us with their struggles. When we have trusted the group with our own questions, doubts, and convictions about prayer, faith, church, society, the members have trusted us with an amazing variety of belief and experience.

In trusting the group with his story, his significant struggles, the leader models trust. He gives the group a present experience of being trusted. By his self-disclosure the leader begins to indicate the totality of life which can be trusted to this group. Such self-disclosure cannot be a gimmick. The group will catch the difference between authenticity and technique immediately. If the leader will stay in touch with what he is experiencing in the group or in his life and share it with the group, his realness will be apparent.

The leader also promotes trust by showing himself to be trustworthy. Whatever a person shares is accepted. The member with his offering is cared for. The other members of the house church are watching and experiencing vicariously. They apply what happens to another member to their own situation. They feel, ''The way this leader responds to persons and honors persons and cares for self-disclosures makes me believe that I can trust him with more and more of my life.''

The experiencing. Because trust grows more quickly with one other or a few others than with a dozen others, the house church provides many kinds of experiencing: in dyads, that is, with partners, in triads, and in quads, within the total group.

1. In partners

    a) Experiencing a trust walk

Everyone finds a partner. One partner closes his eyes and trusts the other person to lead him around the available space of the house and the outdoors. Help the ''blind'' person to explore the world with his other senses—touch, smell, hearing, taste. Be silent during the walk. The world includes textures, materials, other persons, furniture, dogs, trees, earth, and so forth. Use your imagination to give your partner a good trip. After ten minutes (or longer) the roles of leading and being led are reversed. Reflect upon the experience, first in the partnerships, then in the total group. What did you become aware of in your body and feelings? How did you feel about your partner? Were you frightened? Were you tense? Did you trust? What increased and what decreased your trust? Did you prefer to be led or to lead? The trust walk is an experience of trust and increasing awareness of the whole person (body, mind, and feelings). Members are often surprised by their initial anxiety, the relaxation, the wonders of the world around

them which had gone unnoticed, the importance of meeting
another person, and the unused senses.

b) Experiencing a trust fall

Choose a partner relatively close to your own height and
weight. One member stands two feet or so behind the other
person. The front person lifts his arms slightly from his side and
when the rear person is ready to catch him, he falls. *Be sure* the
catching person is ready. Catch him under the arms as he falls
backwards. Share the feelings of catching and being caught and
the trust involved.

c) Experiencing one's control and responsibility for oneself

Everyone finds a partner. One member of each partnership
makes a fist and keeps it tight. The other member tries to open the
closed fist. Even if the fist is opened temporarily it springs shut
whenever the pressure is released. Reverse roles. After both
partners have experienced the struggle of trying to open a closed
fist and the control each one has over that fist, let each take
responsibility for extending an open hand to the other. Then talk
together about the experience. How did it feel? What were you
aware of in your own body and in the other person? Let the whole
group talk about the experience.

d) Experiencing another's humanness

The group is divided in half and arranged in two concentric
circles, each person having a partner. The leader provides the
topic for five-minute conversations, each partner takes roughly
half the time. At the end of each conversation, one of the circles
moves clockwise, thus making new partners for the next conversation. You will need as many conversation topics as you have
pairs. Choose subjects for the conversations which may open
up experiences and feelings common to many, thus implying that
everything and anything is a suitable concern for a house church.
Besides the topics which can be found in chapter 1, we have used:

Tell each other about your job or what you spend your time at even if you don't get paid for it. What has been (and is) your experience with the church? Relate a recurrent fear. What is, or would be, your greatest joy? Which Bible image or parable has most meaning for you? Tell each other about the hardest, most unkind thing ever said to you. What do you like and dislike about your body?

People enjoy these conversations. The topics are real and important; meaningful relationships are begun and each person discovers, to his ease, that he is in control of himself and that no one, especially not the leader, is going to pick at him.

2. In the total house church group

a) Timer history

Each person in the house church tells his history in seven minutes (timed by an oven timer). The leader models this by telling his own story first relating the important parent, grandparent, and sibling relationships of his childhood, the family sense of who they were, his own self-concept, his present family relationships, issues, and concerns. Because this exercise takes a great amount of time, it ought only to be used when the house church has scheduled four or five days.

b) Experiencing common feelings that impede trust

Each person thinks of a secret in his life unknown to the members of the house church. Then he imagines how he would feel if he told his secret to the group. Go around the group and share the feelings you imagined would be yours if you trusted the group with your secret. Do not share the secret. When all have spoken let the group reflect upon the feelings shared. Are you surprised? Are there any common themes?

c) Experiencing the group's trustworthiness

Each person writes on a 3" X 5" card a secret about which he feels guilty. Having never revealed the secret, you don't know how persons would respond if they knew. Place the cards in the center of the circle. In turn, each person goes to the pile and draws a card. He reads the card to the group then tells how he would feel if that were his experience and how he would respond if someone shared this secret with him. After going around the group talk about the experience. Are you surprised? What have you learned about personal responses to guilt?

d) Experiencing unconditional acceptance

This is the ultimate experience of love and trust in the house church. It is not an exercise, done by everyone at the same time; it is work, done by one at a time, as he is ready. He shares his present problems, feelings, incompleteness with the members of the house church and seeks their understanding and help. He entrusts some troubling aspect of his life to the group and finds, incredibly enough, that he is still acceptable. Most of us imagine that we are not acceptable, entirely; that there are some parts which are best kept hidden. To discover that all of one is acceptable, even the worst parts, is to experience joy and freedom unlike anything previously felt. Singing and dancing and hugging break loose; persons care for one another as they have never done before, especially not in church; fellowship becomes real. "See, how these Christians love one another."

A member of a house church wrote us some months later of his experience:

Great numbers of things happened in the house church but I believe the most significant thing that happened to me was that I was accepted and affirmed. But this acceptance and affirmation had some guts to it. First of all you accepted my anger, something I had not even accepted myself. Nobody got up tight when I got down on my knees and beat hell out of that pillow. Nobody said I was evil when I expressed my feelings of hatred toward my father. Second you affirmed me. You allowed me to make my offer to the group. You saw within me the vague stirrings of something good and worthwhile and you encouraged me to use this good thing. After I got home whenever I got up tight or scared I would say to myself "There are twenty people in the world who love me." Somehow that gave me the needed courage to face the task.

Erik Erikson, in his elegant construct of the development of personality through eight ages of man, sees a relationship between interpersonal trust and religious faith.

Trust born of care is, in fact, the touchstone of the *actuality* of a given religion. . .individual trust must become a common faith. . .while the individual's restoration. . .must become a sign of trustworthiness in the community (Italics in original; Erik Erikson, *Childhood and Society,* p. 250).

4. Persons at Work — The Process of Personal Growth

A house church member wrote an account of her experience in a house church weekend meeting.

On the morning of the second day of our house church we were listening to, caring for, and working with Sheila who was crying in anger and love at missing her mother, never really meeting her. I could imagine my daughter making that statement, saying those things to me, and I began to hurt and know that my picture was to be next.

My four pictures were these:

Where I Am—a brown guitar with two strings sprung, producing squiggly, discordant notes.

Where I Want to Be—a blue guitar with all strings intact, producing harmony. Beautiful music could be played on that guitar; vibrant red notes for anger, blue notes for sadness, yellow notes for warmth, green notes for aliveness, freshness. A symphony or a folk song could be played on it, whole and full.

What's Blocking Me—The block was seeing my home as a place to dump garbage, angers from places it couldn't be dumped. Three people facing out, not looking at one another or touching one another. A brown wall. Two people outside the wall were hugging with warm feelings but showing no anger (that gets shown inside the wall).

What Will Remove the Block—a blue house with two loving arms and hands hugging it encircled by a big red heart with all the colors of the blue guitar.

I began to work. I worked as parent-Treva and person-Treva and later home-Treva and person-Treva. I left a part of me outside the door of the home and went into the house in a sergeant stance. An angry, unfree stance, almost exclusively with the kids. Part of me resented the time and energy each of them took, but there was a gnawing feeling that a deeper separation was there, a deeper guilt.

Finally, "I don't want to be bitchy at home and cool and warm and all the good things with others. I want to be real. I want Sallie and Don and George to feel my love, not my orders and irritation."

Then I got stuck. My hands were stuck on my head as if my head had to give the answer. Was it really in my hands? Was the answer somewhere other than in my head?

The leader of the group came over. "What are your hands doing?" He began to press on them, and I was pushing and pressing my head and covering my mouth. Tears began. I was hurting for all the times I missed Sallie, Don, and George. The leader said, "Tell Don how you want to be now."

"Don, I want to love you and show you that and not give you orders. . . . George, you're a fighter, and it's hard to get to you. I have a hard time but I want to . . . . Sallie, I have the most trouble with you. You're the first and the only girl, and I expect so much of you (I expect so much of me?). Your entry into womanhood is scary for me. I want to see you enjoy your womanness, your body. I want to be there to take you through the gate, and it's your trip, your life when you go through. I can't define it for you, but I'm excited for you. I want to hold you on my lap. I want to teach you to dance . . . Sallie, I'm sorry for all the times I wasn't present for you."

The leader asked, "What does Sallie say?"

"She says, 'That's okay, Mom, no one's perfect.'"

As I say how excited and happy I am, Ron notices my hands and says, "Let your hands speak." They go up by my shoulder and begin to caress what feels like Sallie's head and beautiful, blond hair. She seems present to me. As I begin stroking her, in fantasy, I feel a strange sensation in my hands, not exactly a tingling but a movement, like little back and forth movements. "I am feeling a strange sensation in my hands." Then I became aware that I wanted to go home and relate to my children in a new way, to love them, caress them, not dump on them.

As I looked around me at the people in that room, I felt the presence of love among us. Incredible, for we were virtual strangers to one another twenty-four hours ago. It was awesome, and it was real. I cannot explain it, but I rejoice in it. I feel that I am a new person, in harmony with myself and with my family.

There is a fourfold process at work when a person entrusts a part of his life to the group. These stages are recognizable and necessary, and each person will move through them in his own way. A person may move through the stages very rapidly in a few minutes or it may take an hour, or it may start and stop over a period of time. But when a person feels ''finished,'' these stages have been completed.

Out of much house church experience we have derived a model of the process. We know that this model of personal transformation cannot be applied rigidly. Transformation may be big or little and it is not completed, once and for all, the rest of one's life. A sense of completion may occur, and then a person will discover that closure on one part of his past triggers new ''forgotten'' parts which also need to be worked on. Each person keeps his own books. The process is endless. The house church offers members the chance to grow through this process.

Trust is the first stage in the process. When a person entrusts some unassimilated part of his experience to the house church, he has become involved in the process of growth. ''I want to work on . . . a hurtful feeling, a perplexing relationship, an unfulfilled need, an anxious ache, a desire to grow in some respect, a puzzling uneasiness.'' Often this desire to work has been evoked by someone else's story. Persons sometimes voice the concern that they are taking too much time, or surely others are not interested in their story. The feedback usually reveals the opposite to be true; there is a great deal of interest and vicarious participation. One person's trust frees other persons to trust.

Struggle is the second stage. The person tells his story as the church members listen, seek clarification of what he is saying, express their support, and try to understand how it is in his life. Telling the story is releasing in itself and a necessary part of the struggle. Then the members begin to offer ways in which the person can experience his dilemma and go beyond the point where he is stuck in his story. The house church's care and love encourage the person to disclose more of his situation as members report how they are experiencing the person right now in his struggle. Persons hear and see and seek to understand the world from one another's viewpoint. They are present to one another. Such responses allow the person who is working to experience the struggle with his whole being—body, mind, and feelings. No interpretation or solution is handed to him. Slowly or suddenly, he finds it for himself uniquely within his own situation. He must own it, taste it, feel it, embody it.

Awareness is the third stage. The moment comes in the midst of the struggle when the person, often suddenly, sees and feels himself and his situation in a new way. Emotional insight into his dilemma occurs. Of course it doesn't always happen. A person decides to stop in the midst of the struggle, and the house church honors his decision. He can go no further now. He is exhausted, but he feels unfinished. When awareness comes (it may be the next day), the person will often look and talk differently from before. He is no longer at the same point in his pilgrimage. He has grown in his insights about himself and his relationships with others. The person has broken through into a new place for himself. He has turned around, and he sees and feels his situation from a new center, a new perspective. Revelation takes place. A new way of looking at and feeling about his past and present life is revealed to a person when awareness comes. Awareness is the stage where assimilation of what was undigested in the person's past is accomplished. It may be a large or small emotional insight, but it is growth. The person is literally and figuratively in a new place. It may come quietly or explosively, but it is unmistakable. It rarely solves all problems, but it has solved at least one.

Actualizing the awareness is the final stage in the process of growth. All learning and growth result in changed behavior. Emotional insight is not enough. Can the person act differently out of his new awareness? Can he actualize his awareness? Can he act out of his newly assimilated state? Can he act in a liberated, new-being fashion? Since the house church is a small community with all the relational aspects of life in the outside world, he can try out his new-found, emotional insight whenever he gets it. Right there. Right then. Subsequent house church meetings always want to know how the person is doing with his awareness and his new behavior.

These are the four stages in the process of growth. As members of the house church experience them, they become new persons, more adequate, more capable, free to rejoice and celebrate. Hope and joy bubble out, everywhere. Creative thinking about vocation, family, community, service to others, and witness to the world is the natural and spontaneous response of a person who has become liberated from his bondage to some past events. No longer captive to unassimilated experiences nor victimized by his own doubts and inadequacies, he is set free to be a center of love and freedom in the world.

ROBERT: ANGER IS NOT ENOUGH

Trust. Robert, a twenty-nine-year-old married man, asks the group for time. He seems tense, angry, ill at ease.

After listening to several other members talk about their parental relationships, he tells us something of his family history with particular reference to several episodes of his mother's domination and put down. In the last couple of years he has been able to articulate his anger toward his mother in fantasy by venting his rage while pounding a pillow. In direct confrontation he has begun to take stands over against his mother and in favor of his own family. But his exploding rage and his new-found assertiveness have not been enough to free him to live his own life. He is sad and puzzled and unfinished with his ongoing conflict.

Struggle. His struggle to change continues as the house church responds by listening, clarifying what he is saying, and feeding back how they are experiencing him. His voice and body become more tense as he tells his story. The leader suggests that he close his eyes, become more aware of his voice and body, and when he is ready imagine that his mother is present. "Talk to your mother. Say whatever you would like to communicate with her right now." There is a silence of two minutes. The presence of the group and its support is alive and felt. Robert's face becomes quizzical. "What's happening now?" asks the leader.

"I see my mother now and she is crying. I don't know why she is crying."

"Ask her why she is crying. And then wait for her answer and speak for her."

There is a short silence. Then Robert speaks, his voice filled with emotion "Mother, why are you crying?" (Pause.) 'Because I love you, son.'"

Awareness. The young man opens his eyes, looking surprised and incredulous. "That's the last thing I expected to hear, that she loves me. And that's true. I know that now in a new way. I've wanted to fight her, tell her off, and that was necessary in order for me to live my own life. But I also want and need her love. Of course she loves me. And I've never asked for her love . . . and I've never told her that I love her. Ever since adolescence I've just fought with her and blamed her." A transformation has come over Robert. Owning his need to give and to receive love from his mother frees him to respond to all people in a new way. He turns to his wife, "Have I ever told you that I need your love? I do."

She responds with a hug and tears and then says, "I'm glad you need me. You've always seemed so self-sufficient. You haven't seemed to need anything, while I've needed so much. I feel closer to you than ever before."

Actualizing. His voice, his body, his face look soft and at rest. He turns to the rest of the group and one by one expresses his need for their love. With some he is newly reconciled, with others he experiences a deepened friendship. Robert had begun to see himself as a loner, fighting unnecessary battles. He wanted to change this style. He makes a contract with the group to tell his mother that he loves her and he needs her love, a report to be made at the next house church meeting.

PETER: YOU FORGOT TO SAY GOOD-BYE

During the house church meeting the members had been aware of Peter's sadness expressed mostly in his eyes and his voice. His participation with his ideas and responsiveness to others had been appreciated. Forty years old, Peter was known to the group as a successful minister who had moved to a relatively large church in the area two years ago. He had had an exciting ministry in another part of the country for a number of years.

Finally, a person in the group reported to Peter how he was experiencing him, not with judgment or questions, but with care. "Peter, I'm enjoying your presence in the group, but I feel sad as I look at you and hear your voice." There was a silence as Peter looked at his shoes.

Trust. "There is sadness in me, and I'd like to share it with you." Slowly Peter lifted his head and began looking at the group. He told us about his present situation which had great resources and possibilities. The people were responsive. His family was happy here. But he wasn't happy, and he could not figure out why. Throughout this recital his voice remained a monotone, quiet and sad.

Struggle. Someone asked him to tell about his previous pastorate. He began slowly to describe his former church and his involvement with the people in his former community. His voice began to become more animated, his body more expressive. Some of the sadness left his face. After he finished, someone remarked, "You haven't really said good-bye to your former pastorate."

"Of course I have," said Peter. "My family is happily settled here, and I've been gone almost two years."

The member gently persisted. "I know that. But that was a

happy place, and this is a sad place. It feels to me as though you don't want to be here, as though you would rather be back there."

"I would!" Peter quickly replied with feeling. "But I can't, of course, I'm here now."

"Peter, people sometimes carry grief around with them long after the loss or change which provoked the grief has taken place," the leader said. "It feels to me as though you are doing that."

"Maybe I am. I know with my head that that relationship is over, but maybe I haven't accepted the fact in my gut."

"I can suggest a fantasy dialogue for you to try, to see if you can arrive at any other insights. Do you want to try?" the leader asked.

"Oh, yes," Peter said.

"Pick out one of the most important people in your former parish. Call the person by name, say how much you have appreciated the person, and then say good-bye. Let this house church experience your sadness with you and support and sustain you as you let go. A pillow was placed opposite Peter who began speaking to it. He called forth the name of his best friend in the previous parish. "Bill, it's good to talk to you again. You were a great friend. Whenever I needed help I could call on you any time of day or night. Remember the time . . . ," and Peter went off describing a humorous incident, laughing as he described it. "I do miss you, Bill. Whenever I was lonely . . ." There was a catch in Peter's voice, and he began to cry softly. Some of the house church members moved over to Peter's side. All were quietly attentive, listening, caring, caught up in a myriad of feelings and recollections.

Awareness. After a couple of minutes Peter became relaxed and still. Looking up at the group he said, "I had no idea those tears were in me. What a surprise! I have been lonely in this new parish and frustrated. My family loves it here. But someplace in me I've kept thinking about the old parish, I guess."

"Are you ready to say good-bye now, Peter?"

"Yes, I am. I've known in my head that this was all foolish.
There are friendly people here too. I made my job shift two years
ago, in fact. But somehow I have not completed my grief work.
And I know all about that too, for other people."

He stood up unexpectedly. Straightening his shoulders, he
called out Bill's name, and the name of the former church and
went on to say, "You were a great people and a great church. It is
a wonderful memory and the work we started goes on. But I've
left you and I need to say good-bye." With some jaw trembling,
and after a pause, in a quiet, firm voice he said, "Good-bye,
church." Everyone was quiet. Peter's eyes were moist.

Someone said, "I wish you'd say hello to us now."

Actualizing. Peter's face brightened up. The sadness was gone
from his eyes. "My gosh, I never really did that either, did I?"
And he went to every member of the house church, looked them
straight in the eyes and greeted them with joy and hilarity and
celebration. "I'm really here, now. I'm really *here* now." To
everyone's delight, he did a little soft shoe dance.

As so often happens, this provoked a spontaneous celebration
in the house church. Though Peter had been formally installed
eighteen months earlier in his new parish, the house church
members created a rather undignified processional on the spot,
marched around, sang a hymn, had Peter kneel for their blessing,
and gave him the right hand of fellowship. Afterwards Peter said,
"My whole being feels as if *this* installation really took."

DORIS: STOP SHAKING ME

A newly married couple who were present in a house church
shared some of their experiences of courtship and marriage.

Trust. The relationship between the wife and husband and his
mother was very complicated. Don's mother had made things
difficult for Doris. During the six months prior to the marriage,
his mother had tried to dissuade Don from going through with it.
She had decided that Doris was unstable and had spent hours

trying to prove this. Doris felt that the mother-in-law was doing everything she could to destroy her. Doris became tense and took out her frustrations on her body. For weeks she was unable to eat properly, and an incipient ulcer was developing. The situation began to improve after the couple were married. Still Doris was uneasy. She told the house church about it.

Struggle. The leader asked her to close her eyes and talk to her stomach. She was relaxed on her back on the floor.

Doris: "How are you, stomach?"

Stomach: "I am feeling better, but I don't want anything more which is rough. I want smooth things."

Doris: "What's rough, stomach?"

Stomach: "School is rough, classes are rough, my husband is rough sometimes, my mother-in-law is terribly rough. I don't want anymore roughness right now, I want smoothness."

Then Doris said, "I see a light which is quivering." The leader encouraged her to go closer to the light. Suddenly she said, "I am starting to shake." She was encouraged to shake. Her shoulders, head, and torso began to shake gently. Doris reported, "Something is shaking me, Don is shaking me, my mother-in-law has been shaking me." With that the shaking stopped, but very soon it started up again and Doris was encouraged to go ahead and shake.

"Let your body express whatever it has to say." As she started shaking again, the leader suggested that she try the line, "I'm shaking myself." Doris said it very softly at first, and then she said it again and then very loud.

Awareness. All of a sudden her face began to break out in a smile and relax. She shook her head (still with her eyes closed) and with almost disbelief said again, "I'm shaking myself." Doris had tried both lines and had discovered that they were both true. A moment later she said, "I think I'm finished for now." She sat up and opened her eyes. A new softness and warmth and relaxed quality in her features was apparent to everyone.

Actualizing. Her husband, Don, reported the sense of relief he felt when she stopped saying, among other things, that he was shaking her and decided that she was shaking herself. He said, "Now I am free in a new way and you're free. I'll have to respond to my mother and my family, but I am quite happy with your making your own response." Their marriage found new and more solid ground. Doris felt more adequate and confident, more in control of her life.

Doris had felt caught by terrible pressures coming from many persons. Her body had great wisdom with a clear message for her. She wanted to get beyond her dependence upon the persons around her. But she felt trapped. The simple experience with her body which started to shake without her really wanting it to allowed her get in touch with her strength and her ability to choose and decide and take responsibility. When she became aware that she was shaking herself, that others were not really shaking her, she discovered some of her power. From her experience with her body she got in touch with how she could take responsibility for her response to her husband, her mother-in-law, and everyone else with whom she had dealings.

BETTY: I'M WORTH YOUR TIME

Betty and Bill had been members of an ongoing house church for over two years. They had joined after their marriage, and they had found the group rewarding and exciting as their relationship deepened, and they found support from the other members. The house church rejoiced with them when their first child, Carolyn, was born. They planned for Carolyn. They learned about natural childbirth and everything went great. For about six months, Betty was on a "high" as she put it. Carolyn grew cuter and was admired by the community. Betty was a buoyant and exuberant mother.

Trust. Something began to happen, however. The sparkle slowly left Betty's face. Finally, one night when Carolyn was nine months old, Betty said to the house church, "I need your help.

Things aren't right. The baby's fine, but I'm not.'' Her voice was weak and her whole manner depressed.

Encouraged to tell more about her feelings and the situation, Betty reported how consumed she felt by Carolyn, how organized and pressured her life was trying to be a good mother and wife, and how things just didn't seem to be the same in her relationships with others.

Struggle. Then in an even smaller voice she said, "It feels like people no longer care about me as they used to do, they only care about Carolyn. Why, they even greet her first, almost as if I'm not around. I'm just the carriage for Carolyn.'' And she began to cry.

Several hands moved to touch Betty and communicated their support. Several members moved to speak at once as they realized that they had been doing the very thing Betty described. Assuming that a mother is really proud of her child and wants her child to be recognized, they had genuinely enjoyed Carolyn and paid attention to her.

Betty went on to describe how it felt. "I'm nothing but a role—mother, housekeeper, laundress, cook, bottlewasher—I'm no longer a person. I've become nobody, just a role, and it feels like hell.'' Then with her eyes turned down she said, "And I shouldn't be taking all your time right now with all this trivia.'' And she began to cry even harder, holding her head in her hands.

Someone encouraged her. It was okay to feel and share her hurt and anger. After several minutes she stopped. The leader suggested that when she was ready she should get in touch with her body and its strength, raise her eyes, and look at the group members one by one and say, "I'm worth your time.''

It took a while, but Betty finally did it. She raised her eyes, looked at the person on her right, and in a faltering voice said, "I'm worth. . .your time.'' The person responded with a huge grin and a loud exclamation, "Of course you are!''

The second person she spoke to said, "I can't hear you.'' Betty said it again a little louder. "I hear you now, but I'm not sure that you believe it.''

Awareness. Betty looked surprised, straightened up, and suddenly shouted, "I'm worth your time!" The person threw her arms around her and shouted back, "You are and I believe you!" The whole house church exploded with laughter and celebration as Betty continued around the group gathering strength from the responses of the members. She came to her husband last. After she made her statement he said, "Do I ever know that you are worth my time. I've been trying to tell you that for weeks now, but somehow I couldn't get through to you. But the house church got through, I can tell by the look in your eyes. Once again the house church has done what we couldn't do by ourselves. Other people *are* important!"

Actualizing. Of course Betty did not change completely, immediately; but this episode was the turning point. She began to "see" from a new center of worth and to find herself becoming a person of worth apart from her functions as Carolyn's mother and Bill's wife. Acting out of that center, many things began to change for her. She had experienced the acceptance of the group in a dark moment.

Actualizing thus began for Betty. It continued in the weeks following this house church meeting as the members reminded Betty of her affirmation and responded to her in new ways outside the group.

Some Methods for Enabling Personal Growth

In print, the methods may sound cold, silly, or threatening; in practice they are redemptive and healing. This description of methods—which are only suggestive and in no way complete —will help you understand and grow in your own skill as an enabling member or as a leader of a house church. With a little experience, you will find yourself creating your own methods.

1. Listening. A member who claims time in the group is enabled to proceed when the others listen with understanding, acceptance, and love, and respond nonjudgmentally. To have one's story heard is all too rare today. Interpretation, advice, and "that reminds me of my story" are the usual, quick, and not very helpful responses.

Russell had been a member of a house church for a weekend, listening and responding to other members. Finally he claimed time for himself when he said, "I have become aware of so much about families as I heard all of you talk about your parents. I'm reminded that I've always felt close to my mother, but my father has always seemed distant and aloof as though he doesn't love me. I have been troubled by this feeling for some years."

The group listened as he elaborated on some of his growing-up experiences. As Russell talked, the house church began to see that his relationship to his father had not been satisfying to him for a long time, and he was wistful about something that had been missing in his life.

The leader asked him to carry on a dialogue with his father in the presence of the house church and to ask him whatever questions he had about their relationship.

2. Dialogue. A powerful means of facilitating the personal struggle for growth is to put estranged parts in dialogue with each other. They may be parts of our being (our bodies, minds, or emotions—for example, Doris and her stomach) or significant other persons from whom we are estranged. One effective way is to have a person move between two chairs which represent the two parts. The leader put a chair in front of Russell. "Imagine your father sitting here."

Russell told a little about him and then said, "Dad, you've always been very good to me. You gave me everything I needed, a home, food, a college education. You have always been kind to me and polite. But I have one question, Dad, do you love me?"

(Russell moves across to the empty chair designated for Dad and speaks for his dad, who of course is not physically present. But the image and perception Russell has of his dad are present, and Russell speaks out of that knowledge.)

    Dad: "Son, how can you ask such a question? Look at all I've done for you, all the good times we've had, the good houses we've lived in, and the trouble I've taken.'' (All this is said in a radically different tone of voice, rather pompous, authoritative, as if lecturing to a student.)

Russell returns to his own seat.

Russell in his quiet voice: ''I know all that, Dad, and I appreciate it. You provided everything for me. I have no complaints about any of that. But did you, do you love me?''

Russell moves across again.

Dad: ''Russell, I don't know what's gotten into you. Let me tell you about some of the things your mother and I did for you when you were younger, and are still doing for you. It was much harder for me when I grew up. I earned my own way through college. But I've been glad to provide it for you. Isn't that proof of the love?''

Russell returns to his own seat. His eyes fall and look tearful. He doesn't speak.

Leader: ''What's happening now?''

Russell: ''That's the way it's always been. I get that lecture which I've heard a thousand times. He took care of me all right, but does he love me?''

3. Embodiment. ''And the Word became flesh'' is still true today. Our bodies carry feelings and words and experiences hidden away in muscles and organs long after we think we have forgotten them. The eyes, the face, the back muscles, neck, chin, stomach, chest, legs—almost any part of the body—can be holding embedded, unfinished business of our lives, fears, hurts, disappointments, grief. By identifying with that part of the body and speaking for it, we often become aware of our situation in a new way.

Leader: ''Russell, do you feel anything in your body right now?''

Russell: ''I sure do! My stomach is tight like a drum. Whenever I'm afraid or angry I get this knot in my stomach.''

Leader: ''Would you like to get rid of that knot?''

Russell: "I sure would."

Leader: "This house church would like to help. Do you trust us enough to let us help you carry the knot and the burden about your father?"

Russell: "I trust you. You know more about me already than anybody else. But how can you help me carry it?"

4. Letting go. Our generation has tried to be disembodied, rational persons, but deep within us we know that we are also embodied, irrational persons. Russell had thought about his problem for years. He knew all the theories. He had analyzed his problem. But he was not free. He had not resolved his feelings about his father or assimilated his growing-up experiences.

To let go means to "free your mind," to give up the control of mind over body and let *all* your senses help you become aware. To let go is to give up the rigid, controlling patterns and look for new ways. To let go, to be sustained by others while exploring one's life is an exhilarating experience. The house church says, "Let go and let us experience and share your pain, fear, grief, anger." The biblical injunction "Bear ye one another's burdens" can be experienced when a person lets go.

One of the most significant ways of helping a person let go is to ask him to lie down on a rug or mattress in the middle of the group and let the group lay their hands on him. The church has known the importance of touch and the power of laying on of hands throughout its history. Russell lay down and the house church gathered around, placing their hands on his body.

Leader: "How do the hands feel, Russell?"

Russell: "Warm, understanding. I haven't felt so cared for in years. It feels good. When my wife and I hold each other, that's good too. But the knot is still in my stomach." The person with his hand on Russell's stomach confirmed that, "Hard as a rock." Russell had trusted the house church with a significant part of his life. He had let go of his feelings that he had to carry it all alone, that no one cared.

Leader: "Do you want to go on, to get rid of that knot?"

Russell: "Yes, I've carried it too long."

5. *Fantasy*. In imagination we can confront aspects of ourselves internally or take trips anywhere, throughout our bodies or throughout the world.

Leader: "Russell, I'm going to give you a flashlight for your imaginary trip. Take it and make a trip down into your body—throat, lungs, and finally into your stomach. Look around as you go and report to us what you see and what's happening. Let yourself go, be free to be surprised."

Russell started down his throat reporting his experiences. When he got to his stomach . . .

Russell: "I see it over there, a hard, tough, rocklike thing."

Leader: "Go up to the rock, look at it, touch it, describe it to us."

Russell: "It's very hard, gray."

Leader: "Is there anyone else down there with you? Look around and see if there are any faces or persons or things."

Russell: "Yeah. My mother's over there and she's crying and my father is there too, but he doesn't seem to see her crying, he's . . . he's lecturing her. Damn it! And he's lecturing me too. I know I've been asking him for love and he keeps giving me a stone, a lecture. And so I've tried to live like a rock—hard, analytical. I've tried to earn Dad's love by academic success because that's the only thing that seemed to make any difference to him. God, how tired I am of that. I've wanted to cry with Mother too. And I never have."

Leader: "Go ahead, cry with her now and tell her what you have appreciated about her." Russell does this and slowly begins to sob and shake. The leader encourages him, "It's okay to cry in this church."

After a while he stops.

Leader: "How does the knot feel now?"
Russell: "It's softer, but it's still there."

6. *Breathing*. When it is deep and whole-bodied, breathing often allows a person to break through to a new feeling about himself. The breath of life seems to have a wisdom of its own which mobilizes personal strength and drives out unassimilated parts of personal memory. How can the church help Russell complete or finish, or cleanse, or get rid of, or work through, or reorganize, or *do something* which will reconcile him to himself and to his father and to his existence in a new way. And get rid of that knot in his stomach.

Leader: "Russell, our bodies often have wisdom about rocklike things. Breathe very deeply, slowly inhaling and exhaling. Become aware of that hardness in your stomach. Can you see it? Let any images come which might identify the rock."

Russell breathes deeply. After some time . . .

Russell: "The persistent image I get is of my father. He has felt rocklike to me. I want to get rid of that feeling."

Leader: "Let go of the father who lives in your guts. Your real father waits for you in the world, but let go of the 'hard' father who lives in your memories. Continue to breathe deeply and as you exhale open your mouth and let the air come rushing out. If you want to make a sound or shout do that; try to move the rock out of your stomach."

Russell begins breathing far more deeply than he has. All of a sudden he shouts. The church encourages him to shout louder. "You're shouting for your life," they say. And Russell shouts as loud as he can for about five times and then begins to laugh.

Russell: "You know, I think it's gone."

Someone feels his stomach again, and reports that the hardness is gone. Russell has become tender.

7. *Asking for what one needs*. Another important learning of the house church which becomes most useful in actualizing new

behavior outside the group is asking for what one needs. How else can another know? A straight request thus becomes an important immediate experiencing of actualizing, the fourth step in the growth process. If a demon has been exorcised he will come back at least once more to see if maybe his old home is still vacant. Practicing a new behavior is a way of filling the vacancy with new actions, feelings, and thoughts. The house church provides an immediate opportunity for practice.

> Leader: "Russell, why don't you sit up and ask some of your fellow church members if they can love you after what you have shared with them."

After encountering several members and receiving their love and support, Russell hears a recurring theme, "We've accepted you before, Russell, but you have been hard and distant with us. Now we know far more about you, and we love you much more. You have trusted us with some of the important stuff of your life." And then a surprising thing happened. Russell suddenly began to run and dance around the room. Someone asked him, "What's happening now?"

"I can breathe, I can *breathe!*"

"What do you mean you can breathe?"

"All my life I've had asthma. When I was fourteen the doctors told me that there was no longer any physiological reason for me to have asthma, I had outgrown it. But I've never broken through. I just did. I can breathe!"

Three years later Russell remembers this experience as a turning point in his life.

8. *Owning.* There are many methods for enabling each person to take responsibility for himself. Encouraging members of the house church to say "I" rather than "you, we, it, they," pronouns which place responsibility on someone other than the speaker, is a way of enabling important experiencing. Doris did this in the episode we reported, "I can stop shaking myself." Another clue about owning is to encourage members to make statements rather than ask questions. Questions, too, place the

responsibility on someone else. A statement is owned by a person, and there is no guesswork about where the person stands. Finally, to ask members to identify "it" or "they" in their speech is to clarify life in the house church and move beyond the grand generalization and abstractions to personal experiencing.

9. *Checking it out.* One of the simplest and most important ways to discover the truth about a relationship is to check it out. Many of our difficulties stem from incorrect assumptions of "what we think the other person is thinking and feeling." Trust makes it possible for us to check out our assumptions with the only person who really knows, namely the other person in the relationship.

This is the process of personal growth and some of the methods we have found useful. You will be able to add others. Any method for personal growth is useful if it allows a person to struggle with his whole being—body, mind, and emotions—or to break through to a new awareness and, finally, to take a first step toward new behavior.

5. Theologizing

The experience of an individual is absolute. One person cannot deny another's experience. He can say that he has never had such an experience, but there the discussion ends. Truth is phenomenological. It is individually perceived, personally appropriated.

All doctrines, creeds, and theologies emerge from the experience of individual persons; therefore, formulating theology is a secondary enterprise for religion. The primary task of religion is to introduce man to God and man to his neighbor, to provide an opportunity for growing a relationship which is real and seminal. Theology is the interpretation and intellectualization of the relationship. A creed is the "I believe" statement which is affirmed after an experience. A doctrine is a formal, generalized interpretation of a religious experience. It is quite clear that creeds and doctrines and theological statements, no matter how authentic and profound, have limited effect on one's experience. They may interpret experience; they are no substitute for it.

Many people in our churches have agreed to doctrines, creeds, and theologies without having the religious experience which those formulations are trying to interpret. The house church starts with the experience and ends with the formulation. Each person creates his own statement and interpretation; no one tries to formulate another's. This process, the reverse of much of the usual church experience, we call *theologizing*.

It has been our experience that, ultimately, each person's story concerns the central Christian affirmations about human existence. No matter where the story starts, how tortuous or burdensome or perplexing it is, it is *always* a story of the failure of love or of doubts about worth or of covenants which have been broken. Frequently all these experiences are in the story. Many persons do not readily see the ups and downs, joys and sorrows of their own lives in the light of Christian truths. We know our own lives and we understand the Christian truths, but we do not always see how the two relate to each other.

The leadership of the church knows of this hiatus. In an effort to provide an experiential basis for theology, the church organizes many programs of many different kinds for many different sorts of persons. Youth programs and senior citizen get-togethers, couples' clubs, men's and women's clubs, guilds, breakfast clubs, study groups, prayer groups, seminars, retreats—the offerings are imaginative and endless. Often created in response to what appears to be a need, these programs require much time and energy of both professional and lay leadership. Sadly, they often fall short and everyone involved dimly knows it. The church is not able to structure its members' religious experience as it has structured their theology. The authenticity of persons meeting together about *real* concerns and dealing with them in *real* ways is often missing. Attendance dwindles; the program dies. A postmortem reveals that the kind of program offered did not provide space or format in which person's real needs and concerns could be explored. Since most of us feel too busy most of the time, not many will give even a few precious hours of our lives to insignificant or irrelevant activity.

Still the need exists. R. D. Laing pointed to it in *The Politics of Experience*, "We do not need theories so much as the experience that is the source of the theory" (p. 3). Fritz Perls relates an episode which illustrates the same point. "A woman attending a lecture by Fritz Perls asked him, 'Could you explain the difference between words and experiences?' Fritz leaves the podium, goes to the woman who asked the question, puts his hands on her shoulders, kisses her. Laughter. 'O.K.,' she said. 'That'll do it!' (Fritz Perls, *Gestalt Therapy Verbatum,* p. 24).

Persons who have worked through a tough problem or a troubling relationship or a grievous memory in a house church have no doubts about the difference between words and experience. The reality of the group's love and support is unquestioned; the experience of finishing, of resolution, of breakthrough is real and powerful. Authentic and human, agreed. Is it also theological? What does it have to do with God?

Dr. Perry LeFevre develops the thesis that whatever makes movement possible for a person toward becoming a center of freedom and love is ultimately trustworthy.

But what justification is there for calling this mode of becoming normative? I think that the answer is that it is the one intrinsically satisfying mode of becoming and that instrumentally it is the one style of existence which makes possible the deepening and expanding of the range of every other intrinsic and instrumental value. It is the one mode of becoming which not only allows the individual and the community to participate in the creation of richer and more inclusive values and meanings but to be able to draw whatever meaning and value are possible even out of evil, suffering, and death, to deal redemptively with bondage and guilt, to bring deliverance from despair. It is a mode of becoming that keeps man open to the future, that makes it possible for him to change and yet to live creatively in the face of what cannot be changed.

If this case can be argued on the basis of human experience then whatever it is that makes movement in this direction possible is what is ultimately trustworthy. An examination of our experiences of trust will show I think that we are only willing to extend trust in so far as we believe that the other—whether object, person, or institution does in fact maintain, support, or nurture our own real good, and ultimate trust will only be extended toward that which increases rather than diminishes our authentic becoming.

It is possible I believe then to move from experience, to normative becoming, to God-talk. The experience which is theologically significant is the experience, as Richard Niebuhr calls it, of diminution and enlargement, what I have called the dialectic of experience in which trust-mistrust, freedom-bondage, joy-sorrow, despair-hope, guilt-forgiveness, acceptance-rejection, loneliness and hostility-love are strangely mixed.

If this is so, we might reason that whatever it is that creates centers of freedom and love in human life is God for man. Whatever heals the inner conflict of the divided self and releases a man from bondage to self and to the past, whatever overcomes hostility and answers the loneliness of man, healing the brokenness between man and man, this reality alone can be finally trusted. This is creation and redemption of a transcendence that heals and saves, and that creates new good. (LeFevre, "House Church II," *Chicago Theological Seminary Register,* Feb. 1973, pp 41-42.)

LeFevre, a theologian devoted to the preparation of men and women for all kinds of ministry, is convinced that the:

theologian will be particularly interested in those situations where the human predicament has been faced in its starkest form and where men have yet seen meaning emerge, the tragic redeemed, trust validated and confirmed. My hunch is that the theologian will need to look where healing is taking place, in the individual, the group and in society —where brokenness is being overcome. He will need to look to where creation is taking place . . . to situations in which love and integrity are maintained . . . to situations in which men are being delivered from immobilizing or overpowering guilt and anxiety, or from injustice, or from dependencies which thwart growth. (*Ibid.*)

The house church has become a significant style of group life where men and women are enabled to face these issues of existence in their starkest forms. Out of house church experiencing a person does the most significant kind of theological work: he can affirm what is ultimately trustworthy for him. A person comes to believe again because what he believes is grounded in his own experience. Not just knowledge about good news, but experience of good news allows a person to affirm meaning and find hope in his own existence and also in his relationship to other persons.

Toward the end of his life, H. Richard Niebuhr pointed to the need for experience out of which theological affirmations grow.

> I look for a resymbolization of the message and the life of faith in one God. Our old phrases are worn out; they have become cliches by means of which we can neither grasp nor communicate the reality of our existence before God. Retranslation is not enough; more precisely retranslation of traditional terms "Word of God," "redemption," "incarnation," "justification," "grace," "eternal life" is not possible unless one has *direct relations to the* actualities to which people in another time referred with the aid of such symbols (Italics added; H. Richard Niebuhr, *How My Mind Has Changed,* pp. 79-80).

One of the actualities to which people referred was the conviction of feeling that they were saved. They had been introduced to God and to their neighbor and had found a saving relationship. They had also found a new sense of worth. Though weak, inadequate, or denigrated by those around them, they became justified, were redeemed, and filled with grace.

The house church brings persons to many of the same kind of convictions. In the presence of hearing, seeing, and caring friends, a person sees his life anew, reinterprets his life, surmounts his dis-ease and despair, and finds that he is a free, joyous, loving, and lovable person. The conviction grows that his experience is of God and the Holy Spirit. He *knows* that he has been redeemed and filled with grace.

The process of theological reflection, which takes place at the end of a house church weekend, starts with individual experience and moves through generalizations about the experience to Christian interpretation and theologizing. Time is scheduled for individual writing and reflection. One way to do this is to suggest a four-step outline.

1. Examine carefully and in detail one piece of your experience during the house church meeting.

2. Lift out the elements of the experience—the thoughts, feelings, physical circumstances. In other words, analyze it.

3. Relate the truth of your experience to the lives of all persons. Make true generalizations.

4. Theologize. Interpret your experience in whatever Christian terms, symbols, or images are meaningful to you. In other words, describe your experience as a Christian experience.

Out of such processes as this all theology has been born.

The Process of Theologizing

Level One	Unique, personal experience	Experiencing
Level Two	Lifting out the elements, themes, ingredients of the experience	Analyzing
Level Three	Developing theories about the analysis and the experience	Generalizing
Level Four	Relating the experience, the analysis, and the generalizations to the Christian gospel	Theologizing

The ground of all theology is personal experience. Personal experiencing and the personal reports about it may appear silly or profound, crazy or reality based, awesome or tiresome, grand or ridiculous to another person, but the experience is, nonetheless, authentic and unique.

Theologizing has always begun at this level. It was the unique experiencing of Paul, Augustine, Luther, Calvin, Martin Buber, Martin Luther King, out of which their convictions grew.

Level two, the first step beyond individual uniqueness, emerges when a person reflects upon his experiences and recognizes elements, factors, ingredients which he can compare with the elements in someone else's experience. For example, fear may appear as one of the ingredients in a person's experience. His particular experience of fear is unique and cannot be duplicated by anyone else. But other persons may have the element of fear in their lives too. "I'm afraid too, but my fear is like this . . ."

In level three, persons are encouraged to reflect, to generalize, to theorize about the elements singled out of experience. It might become clear to a person that certain psychological, sociological, or philosophical theories or constructs about the nature of human existence are true in his experience. Whatever generalizations and theories the house church members perceive will most vigorously be examined in the discussions which are part of the celebration. Each person will take the generalizing of this level back to his personal experience at level one to test it for truth and usability.

At the fourth level each person views his personal experience in the light of the Christian gospel as he knows it. Thus, each person's theology is anchored in his experience. Christianity, from the beginning, has been a religion rooted in the experiences and celebrations of a community of people. The self-disclosure of God was made visible in the life—the teaching, the relating, the experiencing—of Jesus. That is the meaning of the incarnation. Christian theology was not created fullblown at level four. It was constructed out of the thinking, feeling, behaving —the experiencing—of a person, Jesus Christ, and of his friends and followers. It was Jesus' experiencing of God's love in the face of death, the power of love to cast out fear, to redeem from violence and provincial allegiances which has pointed a way and a meaning for all of life for all men and women.

Too often the church has spent its teaching and preaching time with level three or four, believing that the theology which it explicates is a true fit, congruent with personal experience. Some-times it is, but not always. Each person needs to try it out for himself. Only as he experiences it—love casting out fear, for example—will he be able to affirm it.

This is a common-sense description of the way things are. It does not mean that we cannot profit from the disclosures of God and the experiences of men and women of other generations. The study of the Bible and of church history offers insight and hope to many. It does mean that we in the church must always be aware of level one, where theology begins for each person, the unique personal experience. If a person denies his experience, or if the church belittles or ignores it, the person comes to disregard his feelings, distrust his perceptions, and separate what he professes (the church doctrines and creeds) from the way he lives; he becomes hypocritical. `

Theological Meanings of the House Church Experience

Shared by House Church Members

From experience to theology. The four-step theological reflection was suggested to one house church who enthusiastically spent a full hour writing about their experiences. The leader introduced the idea of theologizing in this fashion:

1. The Experience. Describe a piece of your experience during the house church weekend. Write it in the first person as if it is happening now; for example, "I am sitting on the floor and suddenly I feel . . . I hear . . ." This is the raw data of your experience during our time together.

2. The Elements. From the raw data of your experience, lift out the elements, the ingredients, the themes which are present. Pick out the factors which gave the experience the flavor and shape it had for you.

3. Generalizing. Having extracted the salient facts of your experience, match them to what you understand to be a common experience of mankind. What is the important meaning for all human life which my experience reveals or points to?

4. Theologizing. How does my experience make contact with the Christian gospel as I know it? What is the meaning of this experience? What emerges as of ultimate concern for men and women?

Here is what one member of a house church wrote:

1. My experiencing. The leader has just finished some introductory remarks. I'm pretty confused and I still feel rather strange. He's dividing us into two groups, and my group is asked to stand in the center of the room with our eyes closed and wait for someone to choose us for a blind

walk and exploration of our environment without our sense of sight. I move into the center and reluctantly close my eyes. I suddenly feel alone. I hear people begin to move around. Someone bumps me but does not choose me. My stomach tightens with a twinge of panic. Were there an equal number of people in the center and in the outside circle? Maybe no one will choose me. What will I do then? Sit down or finally open my eyes? But it's just a silly game, calm down. Funny how this silly game feels like reality. I often wait for people to see me or choose me or speak to me. Right now I'm anxious and afraid and I feel terribly cut off from the world around me. Why doesn't someone choose me? Did I look too stern or forbidding in the circle? Did I do something wrong already? Oh, someone brushed my arm and moved away. How long have I been standing here? My anxiety increases and I feel myself beginning to sweat. Someone touches my hand and takes my hand and I am chosen. What a relief! I sigh and I'm surprised at how my body relaxes. I've been chosen!

2. The Elements. Fear, anxiety, tightening body, sense of helplessness and being out of control, waiting . . . waiting . . . waiting, my dependence upon others, my racing mind trying to figure out the future, feeling cut off, worry about how I'm doing, inability to relax, profound relief.

3. The Generalizing. What is important for all human living? It is hell to be alone. We all need one another. In fact, we are dependent upon one another for our very existence. To be ignored is a living hell. I want to be chosen. I think everyone does.

4. The Theologizing. The Christian themes of choosing and being chosen keep running through my mind. There is a specialness and a security in being chosen. The chosen people. Jesus chose his disciples. In his life and in his parables, men and women were chosen.

The opposite of being chosen is being forsaken. "My God, my God why hast thou forsaken me?" Reconciliation is only possible between those who choose to be reconciled. The church is a place where persons are chosen and choose one another.

Another house church member wrote the following reflections:

1. My Experience. After sharing my frustration and sense of worthlessness as a mother and teacher, the house church offered to hold me and rock me and touch me with their warmth. I am kind of scared but I say okay. They lift me up and rock me very gently, then lay me down on my back, and put their hands on me. I feel so warm and tender and cared for. I've missed this. My husband cares for me, I know, but we are married and have a special commitment. All of these other people care for no

reason. I can't believe it. I am so moved I begin to cry. I think of my past and of my parents. I feel myself getting angry with them. "Why did they give me a name which everybody knows is a boy's name?" I begin to share this hurt with the group. "They wanted a boy, I know. I was a disappointment to them and still am. But I want to be me. I'm a girl and I like it that way. I hate my name!" I'm crying and I'm angry. Someone encourages me to say that again and I shout it out."What would you like to be called?" the leader asks. Quickly I answer, "My middle name, Lorine. That's girl, and woman, and sexy."

"Great!" he says. "This house church will rename you. From now on you are Lorine, you are no longer Billie. Say it. Say 'I'm Lorine' loud and louder and louder many times. Make it sound right and feel right to you and make us believe that *you are Lorine*."

I say it, unbelieving at first, then joyously and then enthusiastically. The house church joins me and we shout it together. "Lorine. Lorine. Lorine!" I feel like a new person. What an experience!

2. The Elements. Frustration—sense of worthlessness—being cared for physically by many persons—release through crying—awareness of my name and its meaning for me—a new name—naming.

3. The Generalization. I keep thinking over and over, "What's in a name? . . . a rose/By any other name would smell as sweet." Yet, in my experience, there are feelings of both acceptance and disapproval tied up with my name. There's much in a name. The beginning of change for me will be marked by my rechristening. A new person and a new belonging—Lorine is a member of the Western Area House Church. I guess this is the truth I've discovered anew: one's name and one's belonging greatly affects—maybe even determines—who one is and how one acts.

4. Theologizing. Man, there's a lot of crap that goes on under the *name* of Christian. I've been a Christian all my life and never knew what it meant until this house church. The unconditional love and support and encouragement I have received from these Christian folk have given me new understandings of what being a Christian is and have deepened my commitment to the church. To be named, identified as a Christian is to belong to the people of God.

Distillates. A second way to initiate theologizing in the house church is to offer the members a chance to focus on whatever they are most aware of right now (toward the end of the time together). "Write about whatever experience, image, Christian symbols, biblical understandings, stories, or phrases are important to you now after our time together." People need at least half an hour to do this. Sharing what they have written becomes part of the group's celebrations. Such sharing often confirms experiences for some members when they discover that several persons have written about the same piece of experience each from his own perspective and his own interpretation.

Here are some reflections written by house church members at the close of a full weekend. They are the high points, felt, thought about, and distilled. The four levels are all present: the experience, the elements, the generalizing, and the theologizing.

I

To be able to say "I need" is to be simply open to grace and to find others in the pilgrimage—likewise vulnerable and needing—are the channels of overwhelming, transforming love.

"By grace we are saved through faith, and that not of ourselves, lest any man should boast." This world can bear the demonic if the self is heard. What must be heard is the affirmation that in the eyes of someone who can see us, we are worth saving. The word of saving grace is "I will not let you go."

Trust enough to allow oneself to be vulnerable is the key which opens the flood—the grace. It is a gift—unearned. It is God's gift. He gives it to us through the community of faith.

The house church experience does indeed have kinship with revivalism. The essential, crucial difference is that in the house church each person is honored and lifted up in his uniqueness.

II

We are free—many early Christians were actual slaves, but love gave them an inner freedom. We find the same inner freedom. These slaves of Rome were still chained to their oars. They had changed inwardly, but I had never thought before of how important the loving community of Christians was to them. They and we are free and have the support and care of others. We share our joys and sorrows, anger and tenderness, thoughts and feelings, frustrations and love, but above all and beyond all—our mutual concern.

III

I always thought I understood Bible meanings and Bible stories. Verse after verse comes popping into my mind like "perfect love casteth out fear." New insight came today that this does not mean fear will go completely from imperfect human beings. We'll never know how to be perfectly loving. Fear will be in us, each one, always here in this life often, sometimes occasionally—depending on how much fear was there to start with. The more the love grows in us the less the fear will bother us.

This one realization illustrates anew how our stage in our own pilgrimage—(my stage in my pilgrimage)—changes my *perception* of the Bible message.

I'm grateful for the Good News, and as I reflect upon the story (of Jesus' life and death) it seems to me that I know and feel more wholly the facts I knew with my head—that it parallels each individual's life from the Garden of Eden to the crucifixion and resurrection.

This experience here is like a crucifixion—and may be a resurrection *afterward.*

IV

I have always responded to the verses in the book of Acts that told about the Christians getting together for communion fellowship and being able to experience joy, peace, love, and discipleship with *unaffected joy.* Until this week, I longed for that feeling, but never could really get my hand on the handle. My locked-on *affect* always took charge, and the feeling inside did not match the *joy* look on the outside. I was a captive of the mask. This week the mask was gently, patiently, persistently, and lovingly lifted from my head. I felt bloodied at the time and for several hours afterwards, but right at this moment I can say that there is no scar tissue. I have put on the new man—I am a new creation—I have been born again. I praise God, Christ, and this house church for freeing me in order to let the spirit of love, acceptance, and worth flow in and through and out of my soul.

V

Even though I reject much of my early so-called Christian education I had always still retained my belief in the Scriptures. This was an intellectual something that I had somehow held on to. But this week I witnessed and participated in real "life" miracles. I saw demons cast out—I saw healing take place right before my eyes. It was a vital part of my own personal experience.

I think I also got a handle on what the early church might have been and where their power came from. Essentially—they cared about each other. At times in our group the feeling came over me that we waited on the Holy Spirit—we were of one accord. By golly, one of the group would express a need, and it seemed almost immediately the Spirit descended and then things happened. I have a feeling now I always longed for but could not in my depths own for myself—rebirth after having claimed it for almost thirty years. It was a feeling I always expected from the revival meetings I attended, and finally I have the feeling because of a group of Christians caring together.

To me the experience is meaningful because it happened with the emphasis on Christian love and concern. All my hang-ups with this world and what it can be at its worst and my fears of being misunderstood and giving false information with my body language could be laid aside because I truly felt a group of people caring. In turn I felt I could be free to respond to them, they would know that my sexuality was affirmed and fulfilled in my husband. Thank God I could drop the fear, giving a genuine response is so liberating and uplifting. I feel lifted up!

VI

I never trusted God to always love me, to really love me. I have now learned I am lovable and I need to "let God in." I have many barriers that I have built up through the years which I have to think through.

The one I have seen clearly crumbling is my trust in the spirit of God that is in all of us whether we accept the fact or not. Joseph's gift of making us realize it was there in us has allowed us to permeate the spirit of God's love through our own love. This is what allowed us to meet our needs in a loving way. We were fulfilled as people—females, males without the need to step on others in the process and also accept love from the opposite sex without feeling adulterous and still holding sacred the special sexual bond that my husband and I have. God has purified our love and blessed it!

I just realized what Jesus meant by childlikeness. Through our child comes beauty of love not the rational adult or the critical parent, but the emotional, freely loving child. We all become childlike. I kept wondering whether I can envision everyone as a child.

VII

I find myself discovering some clues to a problem that has troubled me for a long time: Why is it that we know a thing, believe in it, think we are living it, only to have some crisis experience open up to us what it is to really know it and live in it? The clue is that we have indeed centered life too exclusively in the cerebellum and have not cultivated and developed our feeling life anywhere near as intensively as we've disciplined and trained our intellectual capacities. I suppose, reflecting theologically, that it zeros in on the biblical concept of personhood as a total unity of mind, body, and spirit (as opposed to the Greek dualism) and that we are simultaneously linked to God yet totally apart and separate.

I have personally been sustained and upheld for many years by the experience of living under an amazing grace—with all the Pauline ramifications of that. This week has only confirmed and reaffirmed the reality of that for me. However, the added dimension that has come to me with a wonder that makes me weep even as I write is that not only do I need to be upheld and sustained by God, but *why* didn't I realize earlier how much I need to be upheld and sustained by others around me? The grace of my work and the grace of God seemed sufficient, but having experienced the sustaining love of this group, I am hungry to risk myself to be able to receive that kind of sustaining love from all kinds of others and to be an agent through whom a total kind of grace becomes available to others.

VIII

The work of the Lord is done by people—in a loving caring group of people. I am like one of the "sheep"; the flock tries to see to my needs—they try to make me comfortable in pleasant surroundings. They sit quietly and patiently, lovingly listening to my words as I struggle and grapple with grim and frightening and ugly figures—they hold me and rock me or lift me and hug me. They symbolically anoint my head. My cup of gratitude runs over. I feel their constant love and tender warmth will follow me all the rest of my life and will follow us on into eternity.

IX

The house church broke open again this power of the faith in the loving, accepting, forgiving community. We reenacted over and over again the prodigal son's homecoming. We broke open the doctrine of grace as each had the need to share his brokenness and accept the healing of being forgiven.

I feel the experience of redemption of being saved from myself and the dark tarnishings of puritanical concepts that twisted "ought nots" into virtues, of being constructively called into the enjoyment of life's wholeness and celebrating again and again the holy in man.

X

This house church has been an opening up to the possibility of new life, *the new being!* the new being emerging or glimpsed in the middle of all the rubble and garbage of where I am now.

It has a lot to do with someone bearing my grief and carrying my sorrow, with suffering in the way persons listen to one another, look at one another.

It is an invitation, gentle but persistent, to enter a place where for the first time attention can be paid to you and your needs: "Behold, I stand at the door and knock." It is up to each person to respond, if he will.

It is a summons to be on a journey of liberation, from everything that has crippled and bound and limited; it is the indication of our need to be on our own.

It is an affirmation of true community—a sampling of what the church was meant to be, the company of those who are "members one of another."

A fantasy trip. A third way to theologize which honors the unique experience of each person reverses the movement; that is, persons begin with a theological truth, look for its source in their experience, and relate the entire then-and-there experience to the here-and-now experience of the house church.

The group is led through a fantasy trip. Here are the instructions.

1. First, have some paper and a pencil at your side for the notes you will want to make about your trip at the end of it.

2. Find yourself a comfortable position, either relaxed in a chair with your head resting on the back or stretched out on the floor. I want you to relax so you are free to be aware of your whole self and open to being surprised by what emerges spontaneously on your trip. Close your eyes. Tense your feet—and let them go. Tense the muscles in your calves—and let them go. Tense your thigh muscles—and let them go. Tense your buttocks—and let them go. Tense your stomach muscles —and let them go. Tense your chest—and let it go. Make two fists with your hands—and let them go. Tense your biceps—and let them go. Make a face—and relax.

Now breathe deeply from your diaphragm. Slowly inhale—and exhale. Let your body feel its fullness and liveness by breathing.

3. Fully aware of your whole self, bring to the center of your consciousness your most important religious truth. Let it surprise you. Try out truths if necessary until one fits right now. Let all else fade into the background. When you have the truth, savor it, feel it.

I'll give you silent time. (Pause for one minute.)

4. Now going very slowly, aware of what you are doing, take your truth on a tour of your body, to see where it seems to live. Where is it most embodied? What part of your body houses your truth? Move through your body—head, neck, face, throat, eyes, chest, stomach, back, heart, genitals, buttocks, thighs, knees,

calves, legs, feet. If no place seems to fit, assign your truth a bodily home in you.

I'll give you one minute.

5. Look around this place where your truth is embodied. How does it feel right now? (Pause.) What do you see there? (Pause.) Let an image or symbol appear if it does. (Pause.) Are there colors, or sounds or other persons present in your place just now?

(Pause for half a minute.)

6. Aware now of your embodied truth, ask, "Out of what experience did you come to me?" Follow it in fantasy until you come to what feels like its originating moments. Let yourself be aware of that experience again. Become aware of the place, persons, objects, feelings, behavior, sights, and sounds of that experience.

I'll give you some time (pause for one minute).

7. Now shuttle back and forth from that fundamental experience to the present moment. Open your eyes and look around you, become aware of yourself, here and now, in this company. Then close your eyes and go back to your experience again. Then come back to now again. Shuttle back and forth as many times as you need to in order to feel fully present here, now, with your embodied religious truth fully available and functioning in you.

(Pause until everyone appears to have finished shuttling.)

8. When you are fully here, write yourself notes on your journey.

Reflection forms. A fourth way in which we have done theologizing is to ask members to complete the following form on the last morning of the house church time together. After filling out the form, persons share whatever they wish in the celebration period which follows. The form stimulates much conversation, recaptures many of the experiences of the weekend and the meanings which are emerging from these experiences.

Reflection Sheet
House Church

Please record freely and spontaneously your feelings and perceptions of what has happened to you during the house church weekend. Use the reverse side of the page if necessary.

1. What were your feelings and expectations prior to the start of this house church?

2. What did you experience during this house church? (Feelings, ideas, bodily action, etc.)

3. How did your perceptions of other people (significant others, present or not present in the weekend) alter?

4. What potential do you see in this process? (Respond as you wish to some or all of the following.)
   —for re-forming your vision of the church?
   —for enriching or changing your theological under-
      standing?
   —for forming styles of ministry?
   —for relating personal encounter with institutional and
      social change?
   —for learning in theological education?
   —for training for ministry?

Here is one reflection sheet reproduced in its entirety, together with a voluntary follow-up letter from the writer.

1. What were your feelings and expectations, prior to the start of the house church?

Anticipation, hope mixed with fear, even dread. Upon arrival, at first, rejection. I did not know anyone except my two companions, and the others cared nothing about me. The whole project seemed a waste of time, and all I wanted was to get off in a corner and "let the rest of the world go by." I felt a great disappointment; I'd traveled three hundred miles to no purpose! This feeling continued throughout the first session of the house church. I had so hoped somehow I would be able to let down the bars of reserve and reluctance to engage in physical contact. I feared this; it was why I had come. But now they (the bars) were higher than ever, and I was not only physically tired from the drive but almost physically ill from the, I suppose, resentment with the entire group.

2. What did you experience during the house church? (As to feelings ideas, bodily action, etc.)

Just about when I was ready to leave the group—I'd actually planned to sneak out and go to bed—one of them quite casually, suddenly lay down beside me with her arm across my shoulders—it had begun—then in "talking to the candle" (which I was not about to do, it seemed silly) one person voiced the same need to be able to let down, break through. And suddenly I was beside her saying, "Me too!" Later, I asked if she would help me to let go. For the rest of the evening I was much more observer than participant—though an interested one. Saturday A.M. Fred asked each one to express that of which he was aware, and my confidante of the night before said she was aware of great tension and fear in me—that she felt my problem was greater than I would admit. Fred asked if I would share it—and although I didn't want to, and it was perhaps as hard as anything I've ever done—I did. And under his guidance the group "treated me." I'm not now sure of just what went on—but loneliness, grief (held in check for thirteen years) and many guilt feelings were drawn out and thrown away. And my "split personality" amalgamated, and I was shown a new road to walk which with God's help will make me not only a *better* person, but I'm sure, a far happier one. It was a very difficult, almost traumatic experience—but the love and concern of the group and the skill of the leader was such as to make it almost (!) pleasant even while it was most unpleasant. And the result—I am at last at peace with myself and feel that I can be of much more use to others. They made me know I—the essential me—is a beautiful person, and this was news! The ability to express my feelings by physical contact became easier —easy for me to give—but I still felt a lot of touch-me-not when others touched me—I wanted it but drew back. So I asked to be rocked. This was hard to ask for and absolutely horrible for the first few seconds. But the horror left—these were friends—I could trust, indeed I had to! and their touch was loving, kind, firm and gentle, and when they had finished with me, all feelings of touch-me-not were gone and my body, as well as mind and emotions, were filled with peace.

3. How did your perceptions of other people (significant others, present or not present in the house church) alter?

Long-harbored guilt feelings toward my mother and family are vanished. The situation is as it is—and I not only cannot change it—it's not *my* cross to carry, no matter how it may appear on the surface. People in the group whom I at first resented became kindred souls—and my two companions who were already good friends became "very special people." We made a pact to remind one another of what had happened here as the glow fades in the weeks ahead, and this means I now have two friends to help me as I walk this new road.

4. What potential do you see in this process? (Respond as you wish to some or all of the following)

—for re-forming your vision of the church?
—for enriching or changing your theological understanding?
—for forming styles of ministry?
—for relating personal encounter with institutional and social change?
—for learning in theological education?
—for training for ministry?

This experience of love and complete acceptance is what the church should be—but seldom is. This is truly Agape, an intellectual concept not too hard to understand, but I had never really experienced it, though I'd had glimpses of it. The small group relationship—even on a more superficial level—is for me the essence of the church, even though I also love the feel of the big congregation, it takes both! I think every minister should have this experience, and several times, to increase his sensitivity to others, to make it clear to him that he too is just a person, to enable him to forget his "pulpit face" and let his real concern come through.

Saturday, May 30

Dear Fred,

Do you ever wonder what happens to people after you have been with them in a group? You are with so many people for such a short time, can you keep them sorted out in your mind, or do all these troubled souls blend into one great sea of suffering humanity? Because I want to share something great, I'll identify myself—I'm the "lonely widow" with the cool, crisp exterior—or I was! I had no chance even to *try* to thank you for the open doors and the new opportunities I found in the house church, and that's the point of this letter.

I learned, first off, that my problems were pretty petty, and a lot of self-pity had gone down the drain. I knew this with my mind, which is why I never felt I should take the valuable time of such helpers as my minister who have far more serious things to deal with—and yet, I did feel sorry for myself!

And—I am learning to let my caring show—and it must really show, for a friend of long standing said, "What has happened to you—you look like a girl in love?" And I am—in love with the whole world and everyone I meet! And not afraid to let them know it, either.

And suddenly, I've found that there are a number of people who really do care about *me*. I just didn't realize that they did—hence, no more really lonely hours, because people are there if I need them. Even this week (which is usually pretty rough with a wedding anniversary and a death anniversary all within the one week) is proving peaceful, yet exciting. The past is gone—I can remember it with joy and thanksgiving, but look forward, not to some distant day when I will "find my . . . ," but to living and loving each glorious day.

This is all pretty poorly expressed—I'd like to write pages—and words on paper are poor things at best to express feelings. But you will read between the lines and know that I am more nearly the whole person than I have ever been—ever, I am sure. A week or so ago, I'd not have written such a letter—too sticky, and besides you are a busy man! But now!!!

Shalom!

6. Celebration

Twenty pairs of eyes stare at a piece of tissue balled up in an ash tray placed in the center of the house church. Quietly one member ignites a match and lights the tissue. In silence the group watches as it burns brightly at first, then almost goes out as the flame dies. It catches again, then slowly, finally, the whole tissue is consumed. The group watches thoughtfully, everyone hoping that it will burn up completely. When there is nothing but a bit of charred paper ash, there is an audible sigh of fulfillment and peace in the group.

"Now let's sing," someone says. The group scrambles to its feet, links arms, and begins to sing "Amazing Grace." The eyes of the members keep coming back to a sixty-year-old man, in whose honor they are celebrating. His eyes are moist, though he sings loudly with the rest. For some minutes prior to burning the tissue on the ash tray altar, this man had poured out a lifetime of bitterness and regret and confession which he had carried, as he said, "right around my heart."

Over the years the man had prayed faithfully about the concerns which had brought the tightness around his heart, and his prayer had always brought him some relief. He knew about God's acceptance; he affirmed it. But the relief was always temporary. He had decided that his pain and burden were his cross. Still he wanted to be free of it. The people of this house church, some of whom he had never seen before, seemed to care, and almost before he was aware of it, he had laid the whole burden down, right in their midst.

They did not withdraw from him nor judge him. They accepted him and his desire to be liberated from his bondage. The house church agreed that what he was carrying was not all his responsibility, some of it was unnecessary, and the burden was no longer appropriate to his present situation. Most of all, the house church, one by one, had said to him that they thought no less of him as a person of worth and that they loved him no less, in fact, their caring and regard had deepened since he had shared the tightness of his body. He could not believe it. "I've told you the worst things about me, and you've accepted me and loved me. You haven't condoned what I've done in the past—I haven't either —but you continue to love me." His relaxed face and smile were evidence of his new-found joy and peace.

The house church wanted to join him in celebrating. Someone suggested that he breathe deeply and blow all the stuff he had held so long into his tear-dampened tissue which they would then burn. Thus they could together celebrate his victory, his freedom. He agreed that that was a great symbol. He inhaled and exhaled deeply into the tissue six times. "I'm done," he said, "and I've added a lot more which I didn't tell you about. I feel cleansed." So it was that a roomful of people sat attentively and hopefully around a piece of burning paper.

To demonstrate grateful and happy satisfaction in an event or an anniversary is a dictionary definition for "celebrate." For Christians, worship has been the celebration of the brotherhood of man and the fatherhood of God made incarnate in Jesus Christ. In worship, Christians commemorate an event which happened long ago and far away. For some, the whole story of Christ's life, the event, is a little unreal. Not false, not irrelevant, but also not current. After all, two thousand years is a very long time. The teachings and images that were contemporary with an ancient culture half a world away cannot be expected to interpret or enlighten the lives of Americans in the twentieth century. In spite of the fact that the preachers, the seminary teachers, and the denominational leaders maintain that the love and acceptance and forgiveness which Jesus lived and taught is available to every person, many have not found it so, even though they are faithful in their support of the church. For others, the worship of the church lacks celebrative aspects; it is boring, deadly, irrelevant, form without meaning.

Frequently, persons have said during the celebrations of the house church that, for the first time, communion or prayer or Bible readings felt real and meaningful. For the first time, they were experiencing celebrating as worship; they were commemorating an event which was both brand new and ages old.

Worship in the house church is the celebration of liberating, turning-point events in a person's life. It is unplanned, created by the participants out of the experiences of their life together. The leader needs to see to it that bread and wine are on hand and that time is available, that's all.

One reason—it may be *the* reason—the usual eleven o'clock Sunday morning worship service has an old-fashioned, out-of-date feel is that it is the commemoration of an anniversary which no one today has any firsthand knowledge of. When the commemoration of an anniversary has a counterpart in a current event—in other words, when the love which was in Christ Jesus is also experienced in the church community—then worship becomes the celebration of that which is real and powerfully present among us. The long ago and far away language and images of Christianity must be perceived in experiences of the here and now if worship is to be celebration having immediate relevance. When worship is not concerned with whatever is immediate, personal, and relevant among the worshiping community, the church can be written off as a holdover from another age, an institution exemplifying cultural lag, out of step with the joys and needs of people in the last quarter of the twentieth century.

Celebration is meaningful to the extent that self-disclosure is present. When trust becomes the dependable climate of a caring community, when persons reveal their joys and hurts, happiness and pain, quandaries and anxieties to one another and receive one another's love and support, the church experiences a quality of life which is deeper, richer, fuller than the members had ever imagined. Love which grows full and strong, sustaining every relationship within the house church and eventually infecting every relationship outside it, is both immanent and transcendent. It is immanent in that it presently exists in the house church community; it is transcendent in that it is infinite, unlimited, more than and greater than the present expression of it.

The self-disclosure of one person to others, revealing his true nature, sharing his burdens and incompleteness, asking only for others' love and acceptance, repeats on a human level the same process of self-disclosure chosen by God to make himself known. In Christ Jesus, God disclosed himself as selfless, boundless love. He revealed his suffering, his undeviating justice, his power, his creativeness, his acceptance without condition. He asked only for unconditional love and trust in return. God continues to offer man a gift which is priceless, timeless, and immeasurable. When a person truly receives God's gift and accepts it, he, in turn, can do no other than give it away. No one can give something away which he does not have. To love and to accept all others, one must love and accept oneself. That's hard. Most of us who call ourselves Christians cannot, or will not—at any rate, do not—do it.

The boundary line which separates the immanent from the transcendent is both permeable and movable. Whenever any person discloses the concerns of his life to the house church and finds himself listened to, cared for, and accepted without condition, the boundary line is changed. Secrets are no longer hidden, burdens are no longer carried alone, past behaviors and condemnations and griefs lose their paralyzing grip, loneliness is dispelled. In the act of revealing oneself, the love which is of God is known, felt, experienced among the members of the house church.

The one who is disclosing himself, opening his life to others and to God, cannot control the response. All he can do is control himself. He can remain hidden and alone, or he can reveal who he is and what is going on in his life and wait for a response. In all the years of our experience, we have never witnessed a house church response that was not full of love. True, we have estab-

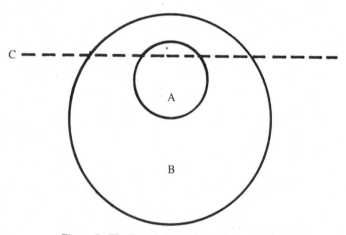

Figure 3. The Immanent and the Transcendent

Figure 3 is a way of visualizing immanence and transcendence in the house church. *A* is any one person and his situation as he sees it. *B* is all the other persons, their view of themselves and of others, and the context within which we all live. Some call this God. Others call it Ground of Being. It is God's world and it is our world. None of us knows all of it, nor do all of us together know all of it, for this world, this space, is more than all our individual spaces combined. *A* is surrounded by *B*. The broken line, *C*, running through both *A and B* marks the dividing place between the immanent and the transcendent.

lished the ground rules of no judgment (see chapter 1), but the warm, loving, accepting response of the house church to one another's hurts or angers or fears goes far beyond whatever ground rules we have established. The person who has revealed himself is often fearful of the consequences. The response of the house church to his story—which he judges to be unacceptable —is unexpected. He is surprised at what he hears and sees and feels and is relieved. And grateful. And ecstatic. The boundary line moves. We have experienced, both as *A* and as *B*, God's grace, love given without condition and without limit. We do not know all the hows and whys of this matter. From our Christian perspective, we believe that the Spirit is at work here. That our words cannot fully describe its working does not deny its presence.

Meaningful celebration—worship—occurs when the following four conditions are present. Under these conditions, celebration will inevitably hold significance for the celebrants, greater or lesser, depending upon the kind and degree of self-disclosure they have engaged in, their imagination and creativity, their sense of freedom, and their previous experience with the traditional forms of Christianity. House church members who are not committed to Christianity will not, of course, understand their experience in the light of the Christian story, imagery, and history.

1. Trust. There must exist a gathered community who trust one another. Some may understand their trust in one another to be of one piece with faith in God. "Where two or three are gathered together in my name, there am I in the midst of them." Others may not.

2. Commitment. The persons of the gathered community intend to be present to, to love, and to accept one another. Some may be aware of the Christian context of the house church—God's self-disclosure in Jesus Christ—and may understand what goes on in the house church in terms of Christian history and teachings. Others will not.

3. Self-disclosure. Rebirth, liberation, new meanings, and growth are experienced within the gathered community as a result of self-disclosure, caring, listening, and response. Some may interpret their experiences as evidence of the Good News proclaimed in the gospels. Others may not.

4. Creative symbolizing. The gathered community creates some significant symbol or ritual or liturgy by which it can recall and rejoice in the common experiences of its life together. Some will discover that the teachings, liturgies, and symbols of the Christian church are pregnant with meanings heretofore unknown and unexperienced. Others will not.

The presence of all four of these conditions enabled the burning tissue to be a significant symbol in the celebration described in the opening paragraphs of this chapter. Of course, celebrations, no matter how they are created or by whom, are not equally important to all the celebrants. But house church celebrations are very likely to feel alive, authentic, and relevant to the participants in that all four of the conditions for meaningful worship are present: trust, commitment, self-disclosure, creative symbolizing. The traditional eleven o'clock worship service is based almost entirely on the first two conditions and devotes little time or thought to the last two. To be specific, traditional worship gives lip service to faith in God (trust), love, and obedience (commitment). Sincere, committed Christians *believe* that God loves them and commands them to love one another; but they do not always practice this love with fellow Christians in the church. Traditional worship commemorates a historical event, rehearsing the stories and teachings of that event (God disclosed himself in the life and death of Jesus Christ), and using the forms and symbols which have long been associated with it (the star, the cross, the candle, the elements of the Last Supper). House church worship is also founded on a relationship of trust and commitment, but it focuses on a present event, human self-disclosure which witnesses to God's self-disclosure of love, trust, and acceptance. Its forms and symbols are created out of the experience. House church worship thus has a greater possibility of being meaningful than has traditional worship, for it grows out of present experiencing.

Is not the General Confession often read in unison in the traditional worship service the same thing as self-disclosure in the house church? No, it is not. In the first place, the confession is general, not particular. It may fit the circumstances of a person's life or it may not. In the second place, since the confession is very unspecific and the worship service proceeds according to an order of worship, there is little or no room for creative symbolizing to commemorate the event.

Confession may be individual and private, as well as corporate and public. Although confession may be self-disclosure to a minister or priest, in which case it never is heard or responded to by "ordinary" persons, the confession receives no love or support from a segment of the Christian community. One expects ministers and priests to accept and forgive even the most wicked and stupid things about one. How one's neighbors and friends will respond is unknown and, therefore, scary.

Celebrations of the sacrament of marriage often fulfill all four conditions of worship and are exciting for all participants. The two people being married publicly proclaim their love and trust and commitment, often using forms and symbols which they have created. The congregation, hearing the vows, often lives through its own memories and promises and pledges its support to the newly married people. Together they pray for God's care and blessing.

Although the congregation in a memorial or funeral service is frequently gathered from many different parts of the country and has, therefore, no firsthand experience of trust among the members they may know what Christian trust and commitment mean and may, through recalling and celebrating the life of the deceased, see their own lives in new ways. A memorial service could well be a significant celebration.

The Lord's Supper, which we celebrate at the close of every house church experience, provides the best illustration of how the presence of all four conditions heightens the possibility of significant celebration. For many people the Lord's Supper has not been significant though it has always been at the center of the church's life. In the traditional service it commemorates events which have not happened to us but to our ancestors. In the house church we place a loaf of bread (unsliced, often home baked) and a jug of wine on the floor in the center of the circle. The leader reminds us that the disciples gathered with Jesus on the night before he was betrayed. Much self-disclosure had gone on among them during their many travels and experiences together. We pass the bread, and each one tears off a good-sized piece. ''This is my body which is given for you'' (Luke 22:19). ''Look at your piece of bread. Become acquainted with it. Smell it. Rub it on your face and note its texture. Hold it up to your ear and see if it says anything to you. Carry on a dialogue with it.'' The leader pauses while the house church studies the bread.

''This bread will not do your body any good even though you have studied it very carefully, unless you chew it up, dissolve it, digest it, and assimilate it into your body.

''This bread always symbolizes, for me, our house church time together. Many of us have disclosed and chewed up experiences of hurt, anger, fear, grief, unfinished business from our pasts, and digested the experience. As we eat this bread let us be aware of what we are doing and how we are doing it. Jesus said to eat all of it, just as we need to eat all of our experience, digesting it or rejecting it, but not leaving it stuck in the throat of our memory.

''In like manner, Jesus took the cup of wine. We say it is the blood of Jesus given for us. For me, the wine also symbolizes the tears we have shed for ourselves and for our neighbor. We have been cleansed. We are in touch with more of our whole selves —body, mind, emotion, and spirit. We are more liberated, more complete, more fulfilled.''

As we eat and drink, members recall the experiences of our time together. Reflections, biblical imagery, theologizing, meanings about the events of the weekend are shared. There is plenty of time and bread and wine. Singing and dancing erupt spontaneously. Laughter and shouting and quiet talking go on all around the room. The peace of Christ is passed by embracing and looking at and talking with one another. Prayers are spontaneous. Persons drink out of one another's cups and feed one another bread.

Many persons have said, "This is the first time communion has ever meant anything to me." The four conditions for significant celebration are present. A people growing in trust and commitment to one another, met in the context of God's self-disclosure, creates new symbols and liturgy to interpret their experiences within the forms of the past.

Although the Lord's Supper remains the central celebration for the house church, there are many mini-celebrations along the way. Members are encouraged to bring instruments, records, personal symbols, creative materials, anything which they feel might help them celebrate. When the responsibility for celebration is shared, a vast range of ideas and talents comes forth.

1. One man worked on his feelings of being trapped by life, caught in the center of strong forces. The group enabled him to work through some of his feelings with a dialogue between his "caught self" and his "free self." As he worked on this dialogue he increasingly realized how he was "catching himself." There were many things he could do, if he would take responsibility for his existence. By the end of his work he shouted and smiled, realizing freshly his own strength. How could this be celebrated? One of the quiet members of the group said, "A snake dance led by this man is the obvious symbol. Let him lead us around and then weave us into a tight circle with him at the center. We will get as tight as he wishes, and then he will have to take responsibility for turning around in the center and leading us out." Everyone agreed. The snake dance formed. There was hilarity at first. Then as he wound us tighter and tighter about himself, a silence developed. When it was as tight as possible, he stopped for almost a minute and stood still. Everyone was silent, thinking, feeling, praying. Then he turned and started to unwind himself and us. A great shout went up. He began to smile and laugh. A snake dance had become symbolically important for his new life.

2. One group adopted the practice of rocking each person and

laying hands on him after some significant experience. The person lay down, the group picked him up to the level of their waists, supporting him with their hands, and gently rocked him. After a minute or two they lay him down and covered his body with their hands for a moment. This practice became their way of caring for one another. It became a mini-celebration. Everyone participated.

3. Another group who adopted the same rocking practice included a man from India as a member of the house church. He began a chant as the group rocked each person. The house church chanted the person's name slowly and deliberately during the rocking. It was a beautiful, creative addition to the form. Several people were reminded of the biblical imagery of being called forth, as Jesus did on several occasions.

4. Frequently persons have come to the house church on the last morning with a poem or a song or some music which they had created late the night before, celebrating their experiences in the house church. It has not always been great music or poetry, but it has come out of a meaningful experience and is more valuable than great words brought in from the outside. Sometimes, songs which are current in the culture take on added significance, and the group perceives them in a new way as, for example, "They'll Know We Are Christians by Our Love."

5. In one house church, a creative dancer was present who suggested that the members dance a celebration. The group was very skeptical, but with her patient encouragement they were freed to try. Each member found a partner, then facing his partner and without words he began to let his body express whatever was in it, reflecting the fullness of the group's time together. When it felt right, each person made contact with his partner and later with others. Beautiful motions began to happen. Bodies expressed and communicated forgiveness, joy, laughter, sorrow, guilt, reconciliation. The group slowly became one large group, all the movements expressing their pilgrimage to this time of oneness and unity.

6. One group wanted to express its independence and interdependence. A member took a balloon out of his pocket and

suggested that the group blow up the balloon. Each person put in a
little air and carefully passed it to the next member. Each person's
breath was merged with all the others to fill the balloon. When it
had gone all around the circle and was nearly bursting, a member
said a prayer, and then with shouts of ''Hallelujah!'' they let the
balloon go. It gave a mighty swoosh, let its air out, and hit the
ceiling.

7. Leadership

The first disciples were frightened and depressed by the death of their leader. They even denied any relationship to him. It felt to them as if the enabling of growth and wholeness which Jesus had offered to the disciples and to others was ended. No one of his followers would ever be able to do what was necessary. However, little by little, the disciples discovered that something had happened to them. They did have some skills to make people whole and strong and confident. They witnessed to the power of love and the presence of the Holy Spirit with such courage and freedom and joy that, without intending to do it, they founded the Christian church.

How did the disciples become leaders? What characterizes leadership in the house church? What must a leader know and be? These are questions we attempt to answer in this chapter.

Jesus was a model to his disciples. It was who he was and how he lived and what he did among men that changed people's lives. Exposure to the person of Jesus, feeling his care and seeing his love at work with all the persons he met, was the way in which the disciples learned how to lead. They had learned far more than they knew. Hesitantly at first, and then with increasing confidence, they discovered that they could empower ordinary folk, even the least among them, to live lives of love.

How do we train leaders for the house church? This question was thoughtfully answered by a student in seminary training. She wrote:

The primary answer is, by modeling a way of being, by *being* and *doing* and *incarnating* the Good News. Experiencing this way of being, rather than reading about it or listening to a talk, is really what is needed.

When you have seen the face of a person who can love, when you have seen a person communicate this love with his or her eyes and touch, you have a glimpse of what it is to *be* loving. We finally come to the edge of language where loving is concerned, for words cannot capture what love is. Love is not only a concept; in its fullness it is an act. If you have *experienced* love, you know what it is.

So step number one in training for house church leadership is experiencing a leader who can love. If we really pay attention to how such a leader works, to how he *is* with people, we can learn many ways of responding. The best way for a leader to learn these is to experience them himself. I have seen and heard and felt a leader:

—accept a person who feels quite unacceptable; "I accept you the way you are."
—express love for the same person, often resulting in a visible transformation. "I love you, you know."
—encourage a person to cry, laugh, scream, dance, jump—whatever discharge his or her body is ready to make.
—hold a person or touch him when he cries or is afraid, assuring him that it is all right to shed tears. "Cry as hard as you want to."
—encourage and guide a person's fantasy no matter how long it takes and where it leads. "I am here with you and so is this church."

But all these techniques remain cold theories until they are embodied. Unless they are used out of an intention to love and care they fall outside the work of the church. The house church leader uses these "techniques" to further a person's experiencing, to open out his life space, to free him from binding patterns so that he can love and become whole.

Loving is teachable only insofar as the leader can *model* it, *be* a loving person. Words about loving cannot accomplish this task for words are only partial. Loving involves whole, living, experiencing persons in relationship.

House church leadership requires a person who knows (can recognize and identify) what is going on within a person and a group; who can act in ways that will be helpful (that is, he has some skills designed to do the job which needs doing); who loves, affirms, supports, trusts, accepts each person of the house church in the same way that he feels God's love, affirmation, support, trust, and acceptance of him. Although the knowledge, the skills, and the personal qualities which are necessary for excellent house church leadership are considerable, we do not believe that only ordained clergy can become house church leaders. Committed Christian lay persons may become very good house church leaders. Many have.

Leadership requires followership; individual self-disclosure requires communal response. So it is that every member of the house church has a listening, responding, enabling function to perform. Leadership, although it resides in a person, does not continually reside in the same person. Any house church member may enable another in working through his hurt or anger or ambivalence. Listening and responding are also leadership functions. Like the first-century disciples, Christians may very likely know more and be able to do more for one another than they imagine. There is a power in a house church which is greater than a cataloging of the resources of the members. "Where two or three are gathered in my name" there is an awesome "more" present. The Holy Spirit cannot be measured, true, but neither can it be denied.

A leader of a house church must *know* some particular things, must be able to *do* some particular things, and must *be* a particular kind of person. It is a large order, but not an impossible nor an unnecessary one. (See figure 4. Model of a House Church Leader.)

Feeling. A leader's feeling about himself, about others, about the church, and about God are fundamental to his leadership. If he does not see himself as a Christian committed to living out the gospel, to promoting it, and to interpreting it, his leadership in the house church will be deficient. He may be able to help others work through their blocks or untangle the knots of their lives, but he will not interpret his activity and the group's life together in terms of Christian community. A leader who does not verbalize his or the group's activity in Christian terms may be a skilled

Figure 4. Model of a House Church Leader

therapist, but he is not an evangelist for the power of love nor a builder of Christian community.

Being a Christian, able to feel another's sorrow, guilt, anger, pain, or joy, and able to love and accept the other with all his lovely and unlovely feelings is the essential quality of house church leadership. The student whose paper was quoted at the beginning of this chapter stated that being, feeling qualities of leadership cannot be learned from books. They are best modeled. We think that is right. If you want to become a house church leader, first become a house church member somewhere and feel what's going on.

The remaining two aspects of house church leadership, the knowing or thinking and the doing or acting, can be learned from books as well as from a leader and a firsthand experience. Do both things. The selected references at the end of this book will provide a good starting place.

Thinking. To become a house church leader, what must one know? The concepts, theories, and current thought lie in these three areas:

1. Personality Theory. The effects of the relationships of mother, father, and siblings. The sex role. The self-concept. Symptoms of stress. Relationship of body, mind, spirit.
2. Christian Theology. A sound theological point of view. A historical understanding and some biblical awareness of the Christian story, myth, and imagery.
3. The Process of Change. Trust, struggle, awareness, actualizing. The identifying characteristics of each of the steps of the process.

The *personality theory* and *Christian theology* which underlie our work in the house church, we have discussed in chapter 2. The process of change is in chapter 4. The reader will find further current references to books in these fields at the end of the book.

The *process of change* is a fourfold movement which begins with a person's trusting the group by disclosing something which is unfinished, incomplete, fragmented, unresolved, or estranged in his life. The group offers ways in which the person struggles with the incompleteness until some new awareness emerges. Then the person is encouraged to act on the new insight, to verify the more finished, complete feeling he has about his life.

A person who would be a house church leader must have experienced this process for himself. Then he will know how it feels. This fourfold process of change is a dynamic one. It is never completed for good; sometimes a person and the house church become stuck and cannot move all the way through the process at any one time.

The goal of the process is to enable a person to integrate or to assimilate the feelings and experiences which distort, impede, or in some way fragment him: guilt, estrangement, grief, ambivalence, self-hate, the suppression of feeling, the denial of the body, hiddenness.

There is a correlation of trust to self-disclosure. The house church leader knows that a person will not disclose important, authentic, gut-level concerns until he feels assured of confidentiality and of acceptance by the house church leader as well as by the members. The leader plays a critical role in the growth of trust. The way he responds to members, honors their contributions, accepts whatever they do or say as worthy of his attention, promotes or impedes the growth of trust in the group. As the leader behaves, so will the house church members behave. If he ignores, pooh-poohs, deprecates, or doesn't listen, if his style is abrupt or acute or abrasive, trust will grow slowly, if at all. Similarly, if the house church fails to extend love and understanding to any member, self-disclosure will be infrequent and superficial.

Self-disclosure and trust are in a tandem relationship; they increase and decrease together. The house church leader knows they are closely related, knows the signs of their growth and deterioration and knows how to promote trust.

Acting. Knowing what to do and how to do it is the remaining aspect of leadership to be discussed. What skills does the house church leader need to have? What must he be able to do and when and for what purpose?

Knowing and doing and feeling are not, of course, separable things. When a house church leader behaves in such a way as to increase trust in the house church, obviously he knows what he is doing and why he is doing it. A skill always includes knowledge with expert ability.

There are three areas of skills which a house church leader must have and which we will discuss in turn: (1) skill in moving a house church group through the processes of a first weekend meeting; (2) skill in building trust; (3) skill in enabling wholeness.

1. Skill in House Church Movement. A house church leader will have experienced a house church weekend as a member before he becomes the leader of a house church. He will have participated in community-building activities, some experiences of growth and change, theologizing, and celebration. Participating in a house church as a member will give one the feel of a house church. Skills and methods which will build trust and enable wholeness are numberless; they can be learned from books or from other group experiences or invented to fit the situation right on the spot.

2. Skill in Building Trust. In the house church each person is responsible for his own life, is in control of what he will disclose and how he will participate. The content of a house church meeting, what happens when, grows out of the concerns of the house church members. The leader has no agenda, no hidden business or time schedule. Everyone learns that time for theologizing and for celebration must be set aside at the end. Otherwise, each house church makes its own schedule. Everyone hears from the first hours together that each person in the group is in charge of his own life. Taking responsibility for oneself is hard to do; believing that a house church leader means it, that he will not probe, pry, pressure, or in some way trick one into doing or saying something which one never intended is hard to believe. Skepticism runs high, scare stories of "touchie-feelie" groups of nudity, and of sexual high jinks are rife. The leader, knowing the societal context of the house church, confronts these fears and

misapprehensions straight off. He says what the house church is not and what it is and how he, the leader, will behave. The house church is like the saturated crystals which precipitate to the bottom of the syrup bottle. It is made up of the same stuff as the syrup, but it is sweeter, more concentrated. The leader assures the house church that he is not in the business of separating the crystals from the syrup or in cracking them open or melting them down. He is there to help them become more perfect crystals in whatever way they desire. Thus trust-building begins.

3. Skill in Enabling Wholeness.

a. Modeling. The leader speaks and relates to others in ways congruent to his theories and beliefs. Of first importance in house church leadership is the *being* of the leader. Who he is, how he sees himself within the Christian community, and how he relates to other persons is vastly more significant in describing house church leadership than the knowledge or the skills which such leadership requires. Although particular knowledge and skills are necessary for good house church leadership, the kind of person the leader is and the love and acceptance which he models are basic. House churches are not anti-intellectual soirées. They are firmly grounded theologically and psychologically. The leader models this grounding. He frequently relates house church experiences to biblical phrases and stories, to Christian history and sacrament, to psychological theory. Every person finally makes his own interpretations and finds his own meanings.

The leader is a member of the house church and, like all members, he works on his problems and asks for what he needs. He does not remain aloof from the process of change; he discloses his own existence and vulnerability. Leaders need love and affirmation too.

b. Listening. The leader facilitates listening and teaches persons how to listen. The leader listens attentively to house church members and he enables them to increase their listening skills.

A husband and wife worked on their sticky marriage relationship in a house church. The members heard their frustrations, anger, appreciation, love for each other. The couple relaxed. At one point the wife said to her husband, "I'm really ready now for you to tell me what I do which most disturbs you."

Husband: "You don't listen to me."

Wife: "I'm sorry if I've been a problem to you over the years, but tell me now what I can do. Don't hold back."

Husband (quietly but determined): "You don't listen to me."

Wife (going right on): "In this house church setting I'm no longer afraid, tell me anything."

By this time the astonishment of the house church members was showing in their faces. The leader interrupted and . . .

Leader: "Did you hear what your husband just said to you?"

Wife: "No. What did he say?" (She was encouraged to ask him directly. She finally heard him. Tears came to her eyes as she realized what she had been doing for so long.) "I . . . I guess I had assumed I knew what you were going to say. Often you were silent and that made me anxious so I would keep talking. And . . . someplace along the way I just stopped listening to you. I'll listen, but please start speaking about what is really going on in you."

The leader suggested that they stop talking for a bit and affirm their speaking and listening nonverbally by caressing each other's lips and ears with their fingers. Gently touching each other became a symbolic act of renewal for their marriage.

Again and again members of the house church report that just the experience of being listened to has enabled them to feel more lovable, more worthwhile. It is not enough to nod your head yes, or even to say the words, "I hear you." The listening which is redemptive is very specific listening, which reports to the person as accurately as possible the ideas and feelings which he has expressed. House church members need training in listening.

One way to do this is to pair members and to ask one person to listen while the other person speaks about something which is of importance to him. The listener does nothing but listen for a given time, say fifteen minutes. The listener puts in no ideas or feelings of his own during that time. He fully tries to hear and feel what is going on in the other person. He does not repeat all that he hears, rather he tries to catch the central theme and especially the feeling edge of the speaker. Sometimes he has to try several times to really catch just the right felt meaning being conveyed. It is this accurate, specific verbal report back to the speaker of what the listener has heard which allows a person to explore new dimensions of his concern. After the specified time, reverse roles.

A second method for enhancing the listening in the house church is to introduce the practice, either for pairs or for the whole group, that no one can speak until he has accurately reported to the previous speaker the gist of the feelings and ideas expressed, to the previous speaker's satisfaction. This rule slows down the interaction, but the members of the house church begin to pay much more attention to one another. In the beginning, persons will have great difficulty remembering what the previous speaker has said. This has been called a wooden conversation. It's easy to see why.

c. Dialogue. The leader perceives ambivalences and fragmentations and helps persons work through them. There is an internal dialogue going on in each person all the time. To let the dialogue take place in the presence of the house church members enables change. The internal dialogue is a conflict; the person is ambivalent and uncertain. Some examples are:

I want to do this, but I do have questions about it.

My head tells me to play it cool, but my guts are restless and anxious.

Part of me wants to smoke, but part of me wants to stop.

My eyes feel like crying, but my training has taught me that wouldn't be manly.

Part of me accepts the equality of pay in the parable of the workers in the vineyard, but another part of me resents the worker who showed up at four o'clock.

My head remembers all the good things which my parents did for me, but my chest is heavy with an unfulfilled longing for their love.

Part of me wants to speak, but another part is afraid.

I like part of my job and I hate part of it.

I love my husband and family, but part of me keeps grieving about my father who died when I was young.

The leader, perceiving a person's ambivalence, proposes a method for clarifying the conflict. Two chairs are placed in the center of the gathered community. The fluctuating person plays both parts of the conflict by speaking alternately from each chair. In one such dialogue, Gloria spoke for the cool-head part of herself in one chair, then moved to the other chair to speak for her anxious-gut self. The house church members reported that they were aware of dramatic changes in Gloria's tone of voice, her body postures, and her gestures throughout the dialogue. After four exchanges between the two parts of her, Gloria abruptly stopped and smiled, saying, "I never thought about it that way before. I feel a lot different over here from what I expected. It's really not so hard as I thought."

The variations of dialogue are endless. The left hand can be one voice and the right hand the other voice. The head can talk with the stomach; the strong guy with the weak; the "good" person with the "bad" one; the child with the parent.

d. Embodiment. The leader suggests ways to relieve tensions and unfinished business in the body.

There is no doubt that fear, pain, grief, and anger live in a person's body influencing his health, posture, movements, gestures, and mannerisms even though he is unaware that the feeling is there. Feelings are not forgotten by being unexpressed; they are put out of reach of the conscious mind, stored deep. Our language has an idiomatic expression referring to this fact, "It stuck in my craw."

Every person is a unity of body-mind-emotion-spirit. The body has a wisdom of its own about what is troubling a person. When someone is blocked in thinking or feeling further into his concern, the leader may help the person release more data by paying more attention to his body.

Tightness born of fear or anger, guilt or shame, grief or anxiety, often resides in the organs or muscles of the body causing pain, chronic disease, disfigurements, distortions, spasms. We are not asserting that all illness is a figment of the imagination. We are asserting that much illness has an emotional component which is frequently causative. Many persons have experienced new body health upon working through their tensions in a house church.

Ted claimed the group's time and asked for their help. In talking about his relationship to his parents and his struggle to become free from what he felt was their insistence upon doing things their way, he sat hunched over in a chair with his legs crossed, his shoulders bowed, and his hand caressing his forehead and stroking his hair repeatedly. After he had told his story, Sam asked him if he were aware of how he had been sitting. He was not. Sam then asked him to describe himself. He began to see himself as he never had before as he reported himself hunched over—in fact, "cowering" he said—stroking his face and hair in a pitying and comforting fashion as if to make up for the many put-down experiences he had had with his parents.

In a dialogue of body postures, Sam then asked Ted to sit up straight in his chair with his feet on the ground, his shoulders straight, his head pressed toward the ceiling, his hands relaxed at his sides. As Ted moved from one position to the other, feeling (incarnating) his two ways of being in the world, he began to smile. He enjoyed coming out of the slump moving from weakness to strength, from self-abnegation to self-confidence. He became aware that he had communicated by his body posture a whole style of life and attitude which he deplored and thought he had renounced.

    e. Breathing. The leader enables persons to let go of their rigidities, their uptightness, their mind control.

Many persons do not breathe deeply from their diaphragms, with their whole being, but breathe shallowly from their chests. Deep breathing has the effect of grounding a person, making him aware of his total body, allowing him to sense the contact his whole body is making with itself and with the world. Shallow breathing goes with fears, guilt, grief, or anxiety. One's body is constricted, rigid and tight, as if the person didn't dare fully live by deep breathing.

There is an age-old wisdom about deep breathing as being a way of being fully alive. Primitive religions, Eastern religions, Yoga, and the Judeo-Christian religion have all taught that breath is life, the more breath the more life, partial breathing is half life. Deep breathing brings a person into the present, relaxes the body, allowing whatever emotions are present to emerge. People are often surprised to discover the relationship of their breathing to pain or anger which often surfaces when the breathing pattern is altered.

Spence was a forty-year-old, successful lawyer. He was always eager to get things done, to rush the house church along. At one meeting the house church members, irritated at his haste and future-oriented style of life, confronted him with their irritation at his behavior. He was, in turn, irritated with himself and resigned to his style. "I'm always living for the future and worrying about how things will come out." He knew that his recurrent ulcer activity and headaches were related to his worry and hurry. "But I guess there is nothing I can do but live with it." His breath was quick and shallow.

Bill, the leader of the meeting, suggested that he go to each member of the group and look at him. Then Spence was to close his eyes, breathe deeply two or three times, open his eyes and look again at that person, reporting anything that happened.

"Sounds silly, but I'll try it." He hurried to the first person, Becky, looked at her briefly and perfunctorily, then closed his eyes, and started to breathe deeply. His body visibly relaxed. He did not stop with three deep breaths, but went on for seven full breaths. Everyone wondered what was happening. When he opened his eyes his face was flushed and his eyes moist. "I'm trembling all over. I haven't felt so alive in my body for years. I became aware that I hadn't ever seen you really, and I became sad. Now I'm seeing your eyes and their color for the first time. You look so different. . .no, I'm seeing *you* for the first time. I don't want to leave you and go on to the next person. I want to sit down and enjoy you right now. I feel as if we have much to say to each other. Sorry, group, you'll have to wait.'' And he laughed and Becky laughed and the whole group enjoyed Spence's new experience of seeing.

He did continue around the group increasingly able to be present, more relaxed, relishing each moment with each person. Spence slowed down and began living in the present. The entire house church experienced the truth of ''more breath, more life.''

f. Fantasy. The leader enables persons to cope with their incompleteness, to recognize their anxieties, to say good-bye to their grief.

We all have fantasies or daydreams in which we are king or the champion or living a splendid, untroubled existence. Daydreams, like night dreams, provide us with some clues about what we hold most dear, want most of all, aspire to be. The leader of a house church uses many kinds of fantasies to enable persons to bring to the level of consciousness some hurt or fear or unfinished business which, unrecognized and often consciously denied, is yet a part of each person's life and behavior. Sometimes the fantasy is a guided trip in which everyone in the house church participates at the same time. Sometimes the fantasy is an individual trip taken by the person who is working on something. Such a trip was taken by George into his body. The leader was trying to help George locate the place in his body and the memory which together produced George's anxiety about doing his job. In this experience, as in many, the leader's use of fantasy included his knowledge of *embodiment*.

George was a teacher, well liked by his students and his peers. Excellent as he knew himself to be, he yet found his thigh muscles becoming very tight and causing considerable discomfort whenever he had to meet a new class at the beginning of a term or perform a leadership function with a faculty committee. He told the house church about his anxiety and his throbbing, vibrating legs.

The leader suggested that he lie on his back on the mattress in the middle of the circle, take a flashlight, and go on a fantasy trip down to his legs.

"George, do you see anything or anybody down there in your thigh muscles?

There was a long silence. Finally George replied quietly. "Yes, I see a little boy."

The little boy was George going off to kindergarten. He had lived in a small town and walked several blocks to school each day. His first experience with school had been very difficult. The teacher had been a disciplinarian and authoritarian figure. She expected the kindergartners to behave. School was not the warm, accepting atmosphere George had known in his home and, furthermore, when his mother took him, the teacher was very clear that the mother should not stay at school, but rather should leave George to work out his problems by himself. George went to kindergarten for several weeks, but he remembered how he would stand half a block from the school and shake before he finally got up enough courage to go into school each day. Even as he told the story, his thighs began to shake again—reminiscent of memories stored there years ago. George would stand looking at the school, gathering his courage, and shaking and crying. Finally he would go to the school and spend his half day, but it was no fun; it was all very serious, and he was very unhappy. He tried to stay home and plead sick, but his mother was aware that he was not sick, so she kept insisting that he go. But he was increasingly unhappy. Finally, after about five weeks of school, George became very sick with measles which meant that he could no longer go to school, and he had to stay home for several weeks. George was not really happy being sick, but he was very happy not to be going to school. When the illness had run its course, he had lost so much time at school and was in such a weakened physical condition that everyone, including the teacher, his parents, and the doctor, agreed that he ought to remain out of school for that year and start over again the following year. George did. The following year, when he went to kindergarten, there was a new teacher. A much different atmosphere prevailed, and although George went with fear and trembling he soon came to enjoy school.

After telling his story to the group, George was surprised and intrigued by the fact that his legs had remembered this fearful experience. In fact, his legs still trembled when he faced a group of students or when he faced his peers. It was not that he was always anxious or fearful, but this memory of kindergarten was still with him; his body had never forgotten it.

Sally, a member of the house church, suggested that George talk with the little boy. At first George was angry with the little boy for still being afraid and for causing him to tremble more than thirty years later as he faced his work. After George had been angry for a while, Sally suggested that he try to make friends with the little boy.

George: "Little boy you don't have to be afraid anymore. I'd like to live with you and enjoy you as a little boy who laughs and cries and is afraid. You no longer have to hide in my legs and tremble. You can come right out and be whatever you want to be."

George (speaking for the little boy): "I'd like that very much. I've been hiding down here all these years, and I would really like to come out and join you."

George: "Well, I would like very much to have you join me. What would you like to do?"

George (speaking for the little boy): "I'd like to come out and play, and it seems to me I haven't been able to play ever since those days in kindergarten. I've always been afraid to come out. You stifled me. You're afraid of me or you're ashamed of me, and you kept me hidden down here in your legs."

George: "Well, that's the silliest thing I've ever heard of, but I think you are right. I haven't let my little boy out, I

haven't let you out. I worked and worked and worked
ever since to try to be acceptable and to earn my way in
the world, and I've very seldom stopped to play or to
enjoy you. I guess I have been afraid that if I let you out
you would do silly things. You might cry and you might
keep me from my work. It seemed to me that the world
wanted work. That's what that kindergarten teacher
wanted. She didn't want any playing or fun in that
kindergarten room, and I certainly didn't risk letting you
out after I discovered what that room was like.''

The dialogue went on. Eventually George the adult and George
the little boy had a reconciliation and a reunion. After the reconciliation, Sally encouraged George to stand up and look around
the group and let the little boy out. He stood before each member
in turn and waited for the little boy to do something. When the
child in George came out, George and the person before whom he
was standing laughed and danced and skipped and ran and yelled
and played games like five-year-olds. As George was completing
going around the circle, someone murmured, "Except ye become
as a little child."

g. Practicing New Behavior. The leader offers ways for
persons to try out new behavior.

In *language patterns* the house church practices straight, honest, open communication. For some persons the language patterns
which communicate authenticity and openness are new behaviors.

1. *"I" statements* are used rather than "you," "we,"
"they," "people." Instead of saying, "People won't like that,"
say, "I don't—or do—like that." None of us can know about
what people will do or say or like; I can only speak authentically
for myself.

2. Rather than ask a question, *make a statement*. Do not place
responsibility on someone else without committing, revealing
your own stand. Instead of asking, "How does that make you
feel?" state how you would feel under the same circumstances.

3. *Check it out* means to check your assumptions about other

persons' attitudes or responses by going around your house church and asking each person individually for reactions. Checking it out is reality-testing.

4. *Ask for what you need* means just what it says. Most of us have learned not to ask; we expect others to know. If the others do not know and do not respond, we are hurt, unjustifiably so. In the house church we learn to ask for what we need, or want. It may be more blessed to give than to receive, and it also is easier, but to be fully human means that we must receive as well as give.

5. *Owning* a statement, an action, or a feeling is to take personal responsibility for it. Rather than observing, "It has become very tense in the group" an owning statement is "I feel very tense." Taking personal responsibility for one's feelings and admitting their existence to oneself is owning the feeling.

6. *Can't* often means "won't." The truth about "I can't stop shaking" is "I won't stop shaking." Personal control and responsibility are never taken away from a house church member by the leader or anyone else.

There are important turning points in this process. Another way the house church leader helps persons try out new behavior is by creating human house church equivalents of the psychological situation a person is in, or wants to be in, or wants to be out of. A person who feels trapped, caught in a box, or isolated, or on the outside looking in can try to get into—or out of—a tight circle-box made by the interlocked arms of the house church members. Arm or Indian wrestling, a trust fall, standing on a chair-pedestal, throwing off the weight of several bodies laid across one—the inventions are limitless. The learning principle which underlies this activity is "You can act yourself into a new way of thinking and feeling more effectively than you can think yourself into a new way of acting."

h. Possessing One's Experience. The leader helps house church members process, understand, and integrate what has happened to them.

The primary way a leader helps a person possess his experience is to aid in the creation of a significant symbol which will forever after characterize the experience. The symbol may be tangible or intangible, a song, a dance, a change of name, an "in" joke or expression, or an image left in the group's consciousness.

Gerry was a person who wouldn't be touched by anyone in the house church. Someone suggested that the members of the house church express all the love and caring they had for Gerry to a small pillow which they then gave to her. Gerry happily accepted the pillow which had become an important symbol of love and acceptance for all the members of that particular house church.

Sol, who had worked through a job ambivalence by exaggerating pitching and catching a softball, received the next week a softball signed by all the house church members. He put it on his desk, a constant witness to a distressing tension in process of being resolved.

House churches have rechristened women who have "turned in" their masculine names for feminine ones; they have learned songs and dances that symbolize some new beginnings or new interpretations; they have created hangings for their meeting house with words and symbols particularly recalling their experiences to themselves.

The symbol is helpful for the recall of the experience; the leader's interpretation of house church experiencing as a contemporary counterpart of church history and a current witnessing of the presence and power of love is critical to the integration of the experience into a sound theology. The house church movement may well become the twentieth century Pentecost.

> "I will pour out my Spirit upon all flesh, . . .
> and your young men shall see visions,
> and your old men shall dream dreams" (Acts 2:17).

"For the promise is to you and to your children and to all that are far off" (Acts 2:39).

Part 3
Recycling the Christian Church—Models for the Seventies

8. The Ongoing House Church

The initial house church weekend can be a founding experience for a group. When the members are geographically close enough to be able to meet regularly, and if they have the intention of being an ongoing community, they can continue to be a support group of care and concern for one another. However, an ongoing house church takes effort and commitment on the part of its members, or it will not succeed. When house churches do not work at articulating and clarifying their contract, they eventually peter out.

Every group, including house churches, operates with a contract if it meets for more than one time. Often the contract is implicit and assumed rather than explicit and verbalized, but it is a contract nonetheless. Groups have goals, procedures, a style of relating to one another; these are the components of a contract.

A house church which projects a future for itself must work out a contract. The members must agree upon their goal, their ways of proceeding, their length of life as a house church and when they will renegotiate their agreement. There is no ideal contract, no model which will meet every house church's needs. There are only major matters to be made explicit and agreed upon. Perhaps at the second or third meeting following the initial one, members will be able to clarify their agreement with one another.

The essential components of a house church contract are threefold and quite simple. Each component can be expanded and enlarged and made more specific according to the particular situation of the house church.

1. *Objectives.* What are the purposes, goals, intentions, tasks of this house church? What do we want to do and to be?

2. *Methods.* How shall we proceed in each meeting? Who will be leader? Who is responsible for food, mailings, convening, hostessing, "working?" How many hours shall we meet at any one time, and how many weeks or months shall we continue as a house church before we renegotiate this agreement? When or how can new members be added?

3. *Evaluation.* How shall we evaluate and when?

Clarification of objectives, specific detailing of methods, and agreed-upon expectations of evaluation free the members of a house church to continue in full support of one another. By knowing in explicit detail what the nature of one's commitment to others is, in time and in relationship, a person can question or clarify or revoke his participation with honesty and openness.

A house church contract can be diagrammed in a triangle. Each point of the triangle is necessary if the form is to be complete; and the interaction between the points goes in two directions.

Without a contract, a house church falls victim to the moods of a given day, domination by talkative members, too much socializing, there-and-then reporting, or dependence upon certain persons. Nor does the group know what to do about the inevitable request to admit new members.

Figure 5. Model of a House Church Contract

The arrow running between Objectives and Methods suggests that the procedures chosen to implement the goals, the means selected to achieve the ends have to be appropriate. If they are not or when they are not, the Evaluation will reveal the failure or incompleteness and will indicate that either the Objectives or Methods were insufficient in some way. Either the house church aspired to do more than they could do, or else the Methods they chose were not appropriate for the attainment of their goals.

A composite case study of a house church which tried to develop a life without making a contract follows. Although this is a fictional account, it is representative of many of the problems house churches without contracts have encountered.

A Case History

Ten persons, three couples and four single persons, began meeting three years ago as a study group. After one year they invited in an outside leader and shared an intensive house church experience. The group flourished under this impetus and in the course of the next year took in two additional couples as members. From the beginning the group had maintained a project of supporting a local retirement home, being on call to drive persons or talk with them or conduct study sessions for them. All agreed that this ongoing project had held the house church together.

The group met once a week in members' homes. Sometimes individuals shared a current concern or problem. Sometimes meetings were social bull sessions. Sometimes these bull sessions were okay, but as time went on, they became dissatisfying.

At least five of the fourteen members had been going through crises of one sort or another. One couple was having a serious marital problem. Members were sharing a good deal of this information and concern outside the group, but the group meetings were becoming trivial and, for some, full of the tension of knowing people were in trouble and unwilling to share it.

Finally, the tension broke when one person asked, "What are we doing here each week? My needs are not being met, and I'm not sure anyone else's are either."

For an hour the members spilled out a whole list of unresolved issues in the life of the group. Members were not asking for what they needed from the house church. The new couples had not been properly assimilated. All kinds of assumptions had been made and not checked out. Many persons felt they could no longer share the real issues of their lives. Trust was low. There were style differences about how to respond to a needy person. Leadership was confusing. Everyone was a leader; and no one was a leader. Some people wanted to start other groups in the church, even though this group was floundering. People were tired of the project at the retirement home, especially those who carried the bulk of the work. Goals for the house church were unclear and not agreed upon. Methods were diverse and not clear. Conflicts had been unshared.

This house church went on through several difficult sessions to build a contract. Evaluation became an acceptable norm for the group. Every member would be responsible to initiate evaluation when he or she felt it was necessary. No longer would the group wait until the tensions had built up so high.

An Exercise for Contract Building

One way of helping members clarify their personal objectives for the house church during a contract-building session is for each person to find a partner. For five minutes one partner asks the other only one question, "What do you want from this house church for yourself?" Whenever the partner stops, the questioner repeats the question. (After five minutes reverse the roles.) Pressing the question is a means for helping each member focus on that which is most important to him.

Sample Contracts

1. A House Church of Lay Men and Women. One house church which began with a significant four-day experience met again for dinner and an evening one month later. Many frustrations were present. The members represented different churches and had so many different obligations and lived so far apart that getting together was a difficult thing to do and required scheduling weeks ahead of time. Still, because they intended to be the church for one another throughout a program year (September through June), they worked out a contract with high morale and much good feeling.

Objectives: to be the church for one another—caring, loving, supporting
to continue personal growth, respond to need
to have fun and enjoy one another
to experiment with the house church process back home

Methods: We will meet monthly. First month for dinner and Friday evening. Alternate month, dinner and Friday evening and Saturday until four P.M.
The hosts will be responsible to initiate "going around" on Friday evening, everyone reporting where he is, what he is feeling, aware of, doing.
Saturday, persons claim time if they want to work on something and choose the person in the group they want to help them work on their concern (to eliminate the confusion of everybody trying to respond to one person).
Present concerns come before socializing, fun, there-and-then reporting from back home.
Between meetings any person can call the group or part of

it together if he is in a stuck place, or he can call on the phone.

We will celebrate the Lord's Supper at the close of every session.

Evaluation: Each time we will ask how we are doing.

At the end of nine months we will look at the total contract and decide whether to terminate, renegotiate, or form a different group.

2. A House Church of Seminary Students. This contract was developed after an initial house church experience in a seminary class. Considerable discussion went on before this pact was finally adopted. Some of the members wanted the house church to agree on some form of social action in which the group could participate as a group. Eventually they realized that individually the members were involved in many groups whose primary purpose was action in politics, civil rights, women's liberation, black liberation, and ecological environmental action. The members decided that they did not want another form of social action for their goal. They also decided that they did not want to specify any particular reading or study material as a goal. The contract they finally agreed upon was both short and simple. It served them well. Although they had outside leadership in their initial experience together, they proceeded on their own with intention and direction throughout a quarter and then renegotiated their contract.

Objectives: Why we are together:
—to be of service to one another, offer support.
—to try out and create tools, techniques for helping.

Methods: How we agree to work on the above:
—we will begin each time by sharing briefly with one another where we are. Each person will have a chance to share before we work on a major concern.
—we will rotate (weekly) responsibility for keeping the group moving. Person responsible will make certain that we follow up on persons who worked on concerns the previous week and will come prepared with a theme and some way of getting into it on a personal level.

—we will give priority to any immediate concern over a planned theme.
—each person is responsible for saying when he needs group time.

Evaluation: We will review how well we are doing with this contract and what changes are needed at the end of the quarter.

We have described in this book the fundamental, basic experiencing of the house church process. Utilizing this process, house churches develop in many different ways and from a variety of contexts. One or many house churches can be formed from the membership and friends of an organized church. They are the "intensive care and training unit" for the larger congregation. House churches have also been formed independently, drawing members who have become disillusioned with the institutional church or never belonged in the first place. Sometimes independent house churches are related to one another through a consultant or a network of such churches locally or nationally. House churches may bring persons together for the founding experience and because of distance they never come together as a group again. The members return to their own communities. Some house churches include the whole family for some meetings.

The variations are nearly as many as the number of house churches. The contract is the necessary instrument for making explicit the objectives, methods, and evaluation procedures of each house church.

House Church Evaluation Checklist

A measure of responsible participation

1. I trust the persons of this house church
very little   1   2   3   4   5   6   7   a great deal

2. This house church is doing and being what I want it to do and be
very little   1   2   3   4   5   6   7   a great deal

3. I feel the support of the house church
very little   1   2   3   4   5   6   7   a great deal

4. I feel responsible for the leadership of this house church
very little   1   2   3   4   5   6   7   a great deal

5. My willingness to disclose myself to the house church is
low   <u>1   2   3   4   5   6   7</u>   high

6. My feelings are
misunder- <u>1   2   3   4   5   6   7</u>   understood,
   stood,   accepted
ignored

7. My sense of worth in the house church has been
belittled, <u>1   2   3   4   5   6   7</u>   enhanced,
ignored,   affirmed,
diminished   valued

Use this checklist anonymously at first. Each person circles the number on the rating scale which corresponds to his evaluation. Then the forms are picked up and redistributed through the group and tallied. As trust builds the house church can talk about these categories openly, but if difficulties have developed as in the case study, anonymity may be necessary.

9. Singles, Couples, Families in the House Church

What goes on in a house church has a great deal of meaning for what goes on in life, i.e., in all the relationships which people maintain or endure or promote and strengthen. The house church experience is a model for Christian living for single persons (unmarried, widowed, or divorced), for couples (homosexual or heterosexual), and for families (one-parent, two-parent, and extended). Let us look again at the model.

The house church is a group of men and women who listen, respond, and care for one another earnestly, intentionally, intimately. They are present to one another, wholly, with all their thinking-feeling-acting selves. They laugh together, cry together, dance together, sing together, eat together. They sit alongside one another, touch and hold one another. They say and do for one another whatever seems helpful or needful to be said and done.

They covenant together to bear one another's burdens. Although a burden often cannot be completely eliminated, it can be considerably lightened by having several people share in carrying it.

Essential to the behavior of the house church is its intention. House church members intend to care for one another, to hear, to see, and to respond to one another. They may make mistakes, they may miss some cues, they may not know what a person needs or how to respond, but they intend to care. Intending to care does not require a special age or sex or physical condition or a particular body of methods or skills. It requires only a commitment. Specific ways of caring and responding are learned later.

The goal of the house church is to help one another get free, free from guilt, failure, sorrow, fear, pain, inadequate feelings, anger, hangups of all kinds. Such feelings, the experiences which give rise to those feelings and the continuing experiences which strengthen them, are big hindrances to being free. They are hurdles to jump or boulders to go around. They do not have to be identified by name or source, but they cannot be ignored. Often resulting from parental or societal or church teachings of what one *ought* to do or be (the "shoulds" and "oughts" we all live under), these feelings are heavy and cheerless and enervating. It takes a great deal of psychic energy to keep unexplored, unfinished, unacceptable feelings under wraps; so much, in fact, that there is little energy left to respond with love and care to anyone. It is an assumption of the house church that everyone has some of these feelings, like knots in a string. Working together, the house church members can untangle quite a few. Certain it is that until the big knots are untangled, or in some way made smaller, persons are not able to do or to be what their gifts, their education, their experience fit them for. They are not liberated. In the language of a theology widely iterated generations ago, but not often heard in liberal churches today, they are not saved.

Each person's knots—problems, burdens, or disappointments—can be understood as evidence of failures in love or in worth or of broken covenant, the theological pegs upon which the house church is founded. If a person feels not loved for himself but for his functions; if he lives alone, as many widowed and divorced people do, and feels left out of the society's care and concern; if a person's worthiness is questioned; if he feels that his sex, looks, working, and homemaking expertise is in some way denigrated; or if a person acts not responsible in his relationships (he is devious and secretive and violates his contracts), then he is unable to relate to others easily, openly, authentically, intimately.

Until a person is able to think and feel that he is lovable, of worth, and responsible in his commitments, he will not be able to love others, treat them as persons who are worth time and concern, remain true and open and responsible in his commitments to them. This psychological principle is well known. It is the basis of all relationships which endure and enable persons to grow, parents and children, husbands and wives. At the roots of much disharmony in marriage and unhappiness in families lie failures in love and in sense of worth and broken covenants. Very frequently marital disharmony is diagnosed, wrongly, as sexual incompatibility which is only a symptom, not a disease. It is real, as a headache is real, but it is not likely to go away by interpretations of personality or instructions in techniques. There is more involved.

There needs to be a new understanding of intimacy and sexual relationship. To know a person intimately is to know the whole of the person, the heights and the depths, the fun things and the sad things, what he has been through, where he is going, and, most importantly, where he is now, what the world looks like and feels like from his perspective. A relationship of intimacy requires self-disclosure, openness, trust, and spontaneity on the part of each person, and emphatic response on the part of the other. Relationships which are ritualistic or stereotypic (i.e., conversations about the weather, the daily news, the state of health or whereabouts of one's children or parents or spouse) most likely are superficial and unimportant. Only when one person risks sharing his anxieties, disappointments, and angers, as well as his satisfactions, hopes, and joys, and another person receives such disclosures with care and concern, is intimacy possible. Such disclosure-response can be a pattern for two people, as in a marriage, or for a small group of persons, as in a house church. Neither a marriage nor a house church will long endure without intimacy, for few people will choose to invest their time in polite, unauthentic, unimportant relationships. Only as I reveal myself to you and feel myself listened to and cared for and confronted by you, can I know myself. Vulnerability is the path to freedom. "I" requires "thou," as Martin Buber's image puts it. To know oneself requires a relationship of intimacy.

Intimacy does not require a sexual relationship for its complete fulfillment, but a sexual relationship does require intimacy for its complete fulfillment. Relating sexually to another without affirming the other's lovableness and worth and the covenant to which the two people have subscribed is to experience the sex act as a ritual, a pastime or a game. There may be physical fulfillment, but only in a context of casual, unimportant, perhaps negative feelings and meanings. Unless there are tenderness, empathy, and authenticity in their total relationship, persons are likely to use one another as objects sexually.

Failure in marriage is failure in the most intimate and the most difficult relationship. The wonder is not the high percentage of marriages which end up in divorce; it is, rather, the high percentage which endure, in spite of many societal pressures and uncertainties. One uncertainty is the roles of man and of woman, of husband and of wife, of father and of mother. They are rapidly changing. Wage-earning and homemaking are no longer automatically sexually defined. Some fathers may be primarily responsible for home and children while their wives earn a family income. Such a pattern may meet the disapproval of the grandparents and their generation. It will be questioned, accepted in some cases, perhaps even emulated by the parent's own generation. It will probably be considered a reasonable and desirable arrangement by the children of the family concerned. In three generations there can be a complete about-face in an individual family. In the whole of society, changes take longer, sometimes much longer.

Both men and women are in the process of finding new roles for themselves in our society, of being liberated from behaviors and expectations which society or their parents or the church have proscribed for them. Thus, making marriage work is not easy or automatic. If it were, few marriages would come apart. If every pianist could perform concerts without hours of practice every day, there would be more concert pianists than there are bookings available. The successful marriages work because two people have committed themselves to make it work. They have made a covenant together.

In the early years of our work with house churches, we were not aware that the processes of growth and change which we are teaching and modeling as a style for relating and responding in the house church had great relevance to and significance for marriage. We had not really thought about it. To everyone's delight, married couples in the house church found new meanings and new pleasures in their marriage, although the knot they had worked on was often not primarily concerned with their marriage. We began to understand freshly, through the experiences of house church members and through our own, that listening, being present, and asking for what one needs affect marriage as deeply as—perhaps more deeply than—any other relationship.

A good marriage, a satisfying marriage, an affirming, supporting, caring marriage has to be created. In order for it to be created, it must be intended. Each person's commitment must be total. If either member repeats his vows with tongue in cheek, if "'til death do us part" carries the unspoken amendment "or til we hit a big snag," the marriage will not last. We are not maintaining that all people currently married should remain so. We are saying that, without the intent to listen, to affirm, to change if need be, to stay in the relationship through thick and thin, many marriages, when they come to a big snag, will fall apart.

We feel strongly that every marriage, with or without children, needs the insight, the feedback, the support of a larger group of caring persons in working through the difficult periods of the relationships. A commune could be such a support group, if its members intend to be more than a financial or sexual cooperative. Most married couples do not live in communes, however, and do need to belong to a larger community than the nuclear family. Arriving at new insights and resolving to think and act differently are more effectively done when the first steps are taken among a great "cloud of witnesses" than when alone or with only one's spouse. The house church can be such a support group.

Two different meanings of love are implied in this discussion. Although the meanings are clearly distinguishable in some languages (for the words are different, such as in the Greek manuscripts of the New Testament), in English both words, *eros* and *agape,* are translated as "love." *Eros* means physical love. Our word, "erotic," finds its roots here. Erotic love depends upon physical attractiveness and cultural conditioning. (The influence of cultural conditioning can be seen in the example of an older man marrying a younger woman. Frequently does this happen, although the opposite is infrequently done.) Love which is *agape* carries no sexual implications. It means love which is timeless, unremitting, unconditional. It is the love which endures all things, believes all things, hopes all things. It never fails. *Eros* is not timeless and it does fail.

On the other hand, *agape* feels heavy and cheerless, duty bound, laden with ought-ness. What marriages need, what the church needs, what all people everywhere need is to love and to be loved unremittingly, unconditionally, and joyously. *Eros* and *agape* are combined. Rarely does a person have such an experience. When he does it is a day to remember, a feeling to recapture and an experience to shout from the housetops.

Joyous experiences do not need to be so infrequent, so hard to come by. We are made both to need love and to give it away. We can do it; Jesus did it. He embodied God's love and extended it joyously and without condition to all whom he met: fishermen on the shore of Galilee, the woman caught in adultery, Zaccheus in the tree. The Christian gospel is a story of incarnation, it is a story of both the long-ago-and-far-away and the here-and-now. In fact, the long-ago-and-far-away part of the story becomes most real and believable and joyous when the here-and-now part is experienced. God's love, in order to be known and felt, must be part of everyday living. Or else it is a myth, unrelated to reality.

There are many ways for a marriage in trouble to find help. There are marriage counselors, ministers and priests, community centers with family therapy programs of many kinds, books, pamphlets, and other printed materials available all over this country. In our experience, the couples who are part of a group, who talk to a group, and receive feedback from a group are most able to perceive one another differently, and to behave toward one another differently. Couples alone in a therapist-client relationship do not experience the concern, the resources, the forthrightness of a group of people. They can discount or sabotage the therapist's responses, no matter how excellent they may be. It is not easy to dismiss an entire group. The cloud of witnesses is helpful for both the therapist and the married couple in trouble.

Children know, sometimes at a very early age, when a marriage is in trouble. When a parent is inconsistent (what's all right today is all wrong tomorrow), or when father and mother have different values and points of view (about the children's behavior, about what is good and true and beautiful, about what is worth fighting for, giving one's life to), or when husband and wife argue, bicker, and fight constantly about anything and everything, or when one parent is unfaithful in the marriage, leaving the care of the children to the other or to many different persons, or when the relationship between husband and wife is chilly, distant, lacking in endearments, tenderness, enjoyment, and spontaneity, the children know. No matter that the parents ignore it or try to disguise it, estrangement in marriage can never be hidden from children. They know and feel when parents are not "right" with each other. Children can forgive mistakes, but falsehood and phoniness arouse their distrust. They become withdrawn or rebellious, either cautious and fearful, or cocksure and insensitive. When they grow up, their own marriages frequently end in trouble as their parents' did.

Fears of sexual involvement and the meanings implicit in touching and holding others who are not spouses are matters that must be confronted and talked through before house church members can extend themselves to one another freely, out of their own human feeling. Our society has many sexual hang-ups put upon us by Puritan and Victorian attitudes which have been embraced by the church. One of these "shalt nots" is about touching and holding, especially between a man and a woman not married to each other. For too long—and it is still true in many places—the only person who can get away with extending caring and concern by holding and touching is the minister toward a person in grief. All other embraces outside the family are suspect.

Only lately has there been respectable scientific approval for what we have felt right along: hand and body contacts are authentic and desirable ways of expressing concern and caring, in joy as well as in sorrow. Such experiences do not, willy-nilly, signal a sexual interest. When everyone in the house church knows that, persons are free to embrace or to hold or to be alongside one another without concern about being misunderstood.

A House Church Cluster of Families

A cluster of five or six families with some single persons and some senior citizens, thus including different kinds of people, could become a house church, meeting every fourth Sunday from ten to four o'clock. The meeting place would preferably be a home, large enough to accommodate about thirty people for six hours. There may need to be cribs and resting places for infants and preschoolers and play space for school-age children. There will surely need to be meeting rooms for high schoolers and adults. Pot luck lunch would be shared. The church building would thus be free for its usual Sunday services and programs for the people not meeting in a house church cluster.

A cluster of families would provide a dependable community for children and adults alike. Although the adults may not agree on the changing sexual mores or on politics or on concepts of freedom and responsibility, they would most likely agree on the virtues of honesty and fair play and against violence and drug use and be glad that their children would come to know some other trustworthy adults. Many families in this nation's cities do not have even that minimal kind of support group. To organize and keep alive such a house church cluster would require some time and work on the part of the organizers, but it would in the beginning provide a belonging for both children and adults, an intimate, at-home, authentic relationship unlike many of the others they have. Once established, families seldom leave their house church cluster.

At a summer conference some years ago our daughter, who was then fourteen years old, was accepted into full membership in a house church of adults. For ten days she participated with them in working through some of the knots of their lives: marriage problems, job problems, empty-nest problems, theological problems. Not once did she feel out of place or not worthwhile in the group. She was convinced by this experience that the church is a group of people who care beyond measure. No Sunday school program had been able to teach her that, nor had her parents, except in a cognitive, intellectual way. Her house church taught her to know with her feelings as well as with her head.

She heard and saw and felt many things which astonished us, her parents. We are grateful that the adult house church members accepted her as an equal. We were quite surprised that she, very young and very inexperienced with the problems and hang-ups and pressures of the adult world, was able to participate with strong feelings of worth and usefulness. Apparently they respected her. The story of twelve-year-old Jesus in the temple took on more meaning for us. In that episode, both teacher-scribes and the child Jesus were searching for truth. Learners together, they gave to and received from one another.

Looking around us, we do not see many activities or programs for children which are bridges between children's immaturities and the world's realities. Most offerings for children are either insubstantial or saccharine or downright wrong. Children's TV and the advertising which sponsors it is a case in point. Schooling may not be wrong or insubstantial or saccharine, but much of it is irrelevant and uncaring. Church just doesn't matter to many children; "Why do I have to go?" It may not be uncaring, but it often seems irrelevant.

A House Church of Families Tell Their Own Stories

A widow. A sixty-seven-year-old widow, Cora Peterson, shared her dream with her house church at their first meeting. Many of the house church members knew one another beforehand; some did not. All lived in the same town. Cora asked the group for help. She had dreamed the same dream many times, with just minor variations, and she wanted to know what it meant.

The leader asked her to lie on the mat in the middle of the room, close her eyes, and reconstruct the dream in the present tense, to live through it again. With increasing slowness and sadness she said: "I'm walking around by myself in the town not talking to anyone, just moving through the crowds. I decide to leave the town, and I start walking along the road leading out of town. Soon I'm in the country. There are fewer people. The road becomes more narrow. I'm walking along alone. I come to a fork in the road. To the right the road leads down and around the mountain which is ahead of me. I go to the left, climbing up the side of the mountain. The road becomes a path with weeds in it. Finally I come to a wall across the road. I search the wall and find a small door at the bottom. I crawl through the little door with difficulty, and it slams shut leaving me on a ledge overlooking a great valley. I'm stuck here. In the distance, far across the valley, I see a golden city. But I can't get there. I'm afraid, alone, and stuck. Then I wake up, every time." Cora was very moved. "What can I do? The dream keeps recurring. I'd like to stop it."

The house church members felt her fear and aloneness and told her so. They were present for her, listening, and caring. The leader suggested that she close her eyes again and with the group's support try to finish the dream.

"How?" she said.

"Go back to where you are always left on that ledge, be there now. Let yourself feel how it is, right now."

"I'm standing on the ledge. I'm dizzy looking down. I want to get to that golden city, but there is no way. I'm stuck. I'm all alone and I'm scared. (She began to cry softly.) I don't know what to do. I can't do anything."

The leader said, "I understood how it feels. But you have some strength you are not using. Look around and see if any possibility occurs to you. We are all around supporting you."

After a silence Cora said: "I sit down. I stand up. I stomp my feet a little. I look around, I can't go up the mountain any further. I can't get across the valley, it's far too deep and the precipice is too steep. I turn around and look at the wall, and the shut door. It looks tight. I'm stuck. . .I'm stuck here." She quietly cried some more, then stopped. There was a long silence.

"What's happening now?" the leader asked.

"I just realized I could go back, if I wanted to." (With a slight smile on her face she continued.) "This is very difficult. I'm prying at the door. It's tight but I think I can get it open. I've got it open just enough to squeeze through if I crawl on my stomach. It's hard work, but I'm through. I brush off my clothes and start back down the path. It's getting dark now but I know the way. Here I am at the fork in the road again." (There was a long pause.) "You people aren't going to like this, but I'm going back up to that ledge once more."

"You do what you need to do, Cora," the leader said. "You're the only one who knows what that is."

"I climb back up the narrow path, squeeze through the little door. I'm out on the ledge again. It's just as scary as I remember it. I don't want to be here. The golden city is way off. I can't get there this way. I turn around and squeeze through the door again. I'm going back down the path. I'm at the fork in the road." (Again there was a long pause. Cora's face is working and moving with many expressions.) "Isn't this funny! I'm very surprised at myself. I *was* going to take the right fork and go on to the golden city. But now I'm not going to. I'm going back to the city from where I came. I'm walking that way now, pretty soon the road gets a little wider. I'm meeting a few people now. The road is almost crowded. I'm back in the town.''

Leader: "Do you see anybody you know on the streets?"

Cora: "Yes, but they are not looking at me."

Leader: "Go up to one of them and tell them where you have been and what you need from them right now."

Cora: "That's scary. That's really worse than being up on that ledge."

Leader: "I know it's scary. We are all here supporting you. Choose someone you know. Call them by name."

Cora suddenly called out.

Cora: "Mr. and Mrs. Carlson! Stop a minute. I want to talk to you."

There was another pause.

Leader: "What's going on?"

Cora: "They stopped. They're looking at me. I'm looking at them. I don't know if I ever saw them so clearly."

She told the Carlsons her dream, how she walked to the mountain, was scared and alone on the ledge, and how she came back. Another silence followed.

Leader: "What do they say or do?"

Two tears rolled down her cheeks, but Cora smiled.

Cora: "They say they are glad I came back. They would have missed me. I didn't know they would have missed me."

Leader: "What else do you want to ask them or tell them?"

Cora quickly continued the fantasy.

Cora: "I . . . I've felt like a fifth wheel since my husband died, like I was in the way. You've included me many times and I've felt grateful. But many times I've been so lonely and I wanted to call, but it seemed like I'd just be in your way. You had too much to do to bother with me. I wonder if it would be all right if I called once in awhile."

Cora began to cry and smile at the same time.

Cora: "They say they had no idea I was lonely. I always seemed so cheerful and self-sufficient since my husband died. I carried on working and joking. They never knew. They want me to call them. They want me."

Leader: "I'm aware that there are other friends of yours in this house church. I wonder if you can come back to us here right now, when you are ready, and tell us what you need from us."

Cora opened her eyes, blinking as if she were seeing something for the first time. She called out the names of her friends, and they gathered around, hugging her and holding her. She asked if it would be all right if she called them. They expressed their amazement about her need. "You never told us. We thought you wanted to be alone. You've got to let us know what you need."

Later in the evening Cora said that it seemed that she was worth something even without her husband. Until she had risked herself, disclosed herself to her friends, and discovered that they needed her and wanted her with them, she had felt useless and alone.

Young parents. Jean and Judd Thompson were members of the house church of the Parker Community Church. Married five years, they were now the proud parents of two daughters. Judd was trying to establish himself in a television-electronic business and was working a "twenty-six-hour day and an eight-day week" as Jean put it. He had invested all the money he could borrow in the business and needed desperately to succeed. Jean spent all her days and most evenings washing, cooking, cleaning, marketing, and mothering the two little girls. She had no money for household help or for a sitter other than the occasional evening which she and Judd spent with friends. She was hurt and she was angry. Nothing in her education or her courtship had prepared her for the aloneness and the constant requirements of mothering and homemaking which she felt hemmed her in. She had had a career as a supervising nurse before her marriage, a career she feared she could never return to because nursing practice had changed radically in the five years since she had left. She told the house church that she felt like a function, a door mat, a hotel operator. Anyone who wanted to could do the work she did. Her worth was in no way related to her uniqueness or individuality.

She said, sadly, that she had asked Judd to set aside one night a week, any night, for just the two of them. She felt that having a night scheduled, like an old-fashioned date, would help her with the boredom and everydayness of her life. Judd couldn't—or wouldn't—do it. He said he tried, but something always came up. Experiencing again her frustration and aloneness, Jean began to cry. It seemed to her that their sex life was no different from the rest of their life. Judd came home late and they were both tired, but there was little time for genuine relaxation and enjoyment of each other, for they both had to get some sleep before the early-waking baby girls called them to their respective jobs. So in their sexual relations too, Jean said she was a function, not a person. Judd turned over and went to sleep, soundly and indifferently. Jean was wakeful most of the night; she would finally fall asleep a couple of hours before she had to get up.

The house church listened with care and concern to Jean's story. They asked some questions of clarification of Jean and Judd, and together they all worked out some strategies which they hoped would be helpful to the couple. They made a contract which summarized their convictions and expectations which ran like this: "Since love needs to be nourished, and since nourishment takes time, Jean and Judd shall have at least one four-hour date each week; morning, noon, or night. If one's job and/or one's children take precedence over one's marriage, the couple is growing apart, Jean and Judd shall make a report to this house church in one month."

How Jean and Judd were to schedule this time together was left up to them. Jean began to understand the pressures on Judd to succeed, to pay back his borrowed money, to show both his parents and Jean's that he could provide comfortably for his family if he were given the time. A house church member who lived across the town volunteered to take care of the little girls in her home on Friday of each week. Her offer was gratefully accepted, and Jean and Judd began planning their weekly "date."

At subsequent house church meetings, the Thompsons reported on their progress with the contract. They had increased their joy together and their appreciation of each other and had discovered new levels of communication which they had never expected were possible. Although they knew that they would face many other problems, they had discovered that they could face them together. Their communication had vastly improved. They had begun to share their feelings and expectations in a hopeful and confident way instead of playing games of power and revenge.

A Divorcee. Increasing numbers of persons in our society are divorced. Lonely and feeling rejected, the women—especially those in their forties and fifties—frequently have a hard time finding a job and a social niche in our society. Men and women alike often carry much bitterness and pain which keeps intruding in subsequent relationships, distorts them, sometimes destroys them.

Sheila writes of her experience in the present tense.

I've been feeling a number of things rising in me. I think that the need to speak of my marriage is growing. . . . I'm glad to be sitting near Carl. I trust him. I know he will try to help me if I choose to talk about my marriage. I am remembering how it was to be married in 1968 and 1969 and 1970; the sort of constant suppressed panic about things being really wrong with Alex (husband). Knowing he didn't like my body too much. Knowing he wanted to spend time with other women. I was scared to admit any of the fear, and a lot of energy went toward perpetuating the myth that things were okay. I'd write home only on good days.

Back in college I felt some queer obligation to maintain the myth that I was always strong and independent and invincible. To the grandparents and even to my friends, I played that person, and with Alex I just said less and less. But then, following our divorce, I collapsed with confusion and despair and lack of food and sleep, and the whole Gibraltar myth cracked wide open and fell apart. Slowly from there I returned to health and spirits, but it was only because there were several dear people willing to help me and give me back the kind of responsibility I thought I'd lost forever.

But these first weeks in this new town, with these new friends, I have been feeling some fear that the old myth would reinstate itself. And when I wondered if Sheila-the-competent-woman would become my role here,

I shuddered. Some of my behavior *is* able and decisive, but that's not all of who I am. Will the tender parts of me show? When can I let them show? Today maybe? Here?

It's my turn, and I'm telling the whole story. . . . The leader suggests I have a talk with Alex, but the pain comes welling up and I cannot speak. I'm crying. I feel wrenched inside. I cannot talk with Alex now, but I can imagine our small, gray house on Kennedy Avenue. I am remembering being there and it's early January, 1971, and I am telling Alex again how left out I felt and sad and angry when he told me he'd been sleeping with our friend Kitty and would still be doing so if he could. I feel violated and puzzled, and he seems confused and puzzled and at times indifferent. The memory is very clear. I can see him there in his chair in the bedroom. I am standing up and my face is very contorted and I am crying and hurt. He is sitting there looking at me. He looks uncomfortable and distant, like he'd rather be somewhere else. I tell the house church what it felt like then, . . . how I took a large pillow and ripped it, feeling like it was me being ripped open. I did feel ripped apart, and I am telling this scene with the feather-guts flying everywhere to the house church, particularly to Frank. He has edged his way to me from across the room, and now his face is shining with care in front of me, and he takes both my hands in his hands and holds on, and I let the crying come, and he puts his arm around my shoulders and holds me as I cry.

Something is moving inside me! So many times before I described the split from Alex as a drifting apart from each other, a mutual dispassionate decision to part. . . . That wasn't it at all! Now I am giving these people here a true description. My divorce was not and is not a matter of indifference to me. It was a thing growing over many months of feeling lonely and out of touch with anything, and feeling unloved and unloving. The revelation about Kitty sort of pushed it over the edge, but it was a whole lot of hurt for a long time. It still hurts. But somehow now it's lighter. Frank's presence has something to do with it. . . . Janet is bringing me some tissue. Goodness, I feel better. I have told these people . . .some of the very painful things in my life, and they are here now looking at my face with concern. I feel that I can tell them now that I need them. I am saying it. I need you. I am not just a strong thing. I am softness, too, and vulnerability. I care and I hurt and I need. I need you now. For many years I thought I was supposed to be self-sufficient. I am not, I need you.

I sense Jesus . . . here, and it is not as hard to speak as I thought. The others can hear, too, and that's important for it is something I need to tell them all. I am saying I hear God's calling to me, sometimes so strong I don't know what to do. I hear Frank talking about God, too. He says Christ's name with great love and no apology. And Bud is saying too how much he loves God. Oh, I feel like rejoicing now. Two people are saying to me, "I hear you. I feel such love as you do. Let's talk about it. Let's share our love for God." And we are. Something has begun.

Parents of teen-agers. The two most stressful periods of parenthood are when children are pre-schoolers and when they are adolescents. Especially at those times, but also at the in-between times, families need other families in the church to know and be with. The Browns are parents of adolescents.

Laura and Henry Brown are experiencing much hurt and anxiety in relation to the behavior, the friends, and the values of their teen-aged sons, one a senior in high school, the other a junior. The boys had taken to smoking pot, playing poker, riding around in others' cars, and, from their parents' point of view, violating many of the standards of behavior Laura and Henry subscribe to. Henry had commanded Steve, the junior son, to stop associating with his particular group of friends in one stormy session which resulted in Steve's running away from home for several days. Duane, the older son, was the source of even more anxiety, for he said very little, went his own way, and asked for no help with anything. Laura and Henry feared that if they were too strict about the boys' hours and friends and habits they would drive them into the very life they wanted to forbid. On the other hand, if they were too permissive—which they felt they had been—they would feel immensely guilty for having not acted as responsible parents should. Laura wrote of her experience at the end of a house church meeting.

Suddenly I knew I couldn't carry this load any longer. I told the house church of my anguish. Bertha and Walter had shared so much about their sons and their pain with selective service and war, I was reminded over and over again of our distress with our sons and I felt sadder and sadder. The house church asked questions—about curfew, drugs, allowances, church relationship, school pressures, peer group standards. They seemed to understand how heavy it was for me.

I don't know how it happened, or in what order. I sat in two chairs, alternately, and played two roles, myself and one of my sons. I remembered many hard experiences with my long-dead father and I beat them all out of me. Henry and I talked together about our relationship and I discovered that I was relating to our sons as I thought he wanted me to. Since I didn't know what Henry would have done, I was uncertain and the boys knew it.

Somehow I got unhooked. Was it anger vented on the pillow, or the tears of pain and feeling sorry for myself or the house church's steady listening and responding and not letting me go? Someone asked me how I felt about myself.

"A failure as a mother of boys."

"Why?"

"Because they are, in many ways, not what I had imagined they would be."

"You feel responsible for what they are doing?"

"Yes, shouldn't I? The law holds me responsible."

Patiently the house church stayed with me, arguing, questioning, reflecting, analyzing, sharing their feelings about me and my relationships to them. . . . I'm so grateful. My burden is lightened. I am not certain how the boys will come out, but Henry and I are much more together than we have been for many years, and I feel as though I've let go of a big load. Not that what happens to our children doesn't matter. It does. But I no longer feel so much responsibility and pain. Hallelujah!

Parents and an empty nest. What is it to be a man, a husband, a father, a woman, a wife, a mother? Certain it is that there is no one, clearly prescribed pattern. The roles of men and women, and consequently of boys and girls, are changing greatly and rapidly. For those of us who have accepted no single clearly defined model, the uncertainties and conflicts we endure and provoke are endless. The lives of Tom and Abby Jones reveal the conflict of roles they have experienced throughout their marriage.

Tom and Abby Jones, now in their fifties, were married in college. Tom received his B.A. and went on to a master's degree in business administration. Abby quit college at the end of her sophomore year and took a job as a receptionist in a doctors' clinic.

They recalled, with humor, the problem they had had with the family washing in the early years of their marriage. In Abby's home, her mother had always done the family washing on Monday morning. So did Abby. In Tom's family, his father had always done the washing on Monday night, after he had come home from work. So Tom tried to do the same thing. Of course he couldn't because the washing had already been done. Tom felt terrible, he had been remiss. Abby felt terrible for making Tom feel terrible. So they agreed to accept Tom's husband-wife pattern; Tom did the washing Monday nights after work, for two weeks. Then Abby, feeling miserable about herself, beat him to it. She did the washing Monday morning. It was apparent to both of them that whoever did the washing made the other one feel bad.

They succeeded, however, in establishing a family pattern of breakfast that was helpful to a growing family. While Abby was dressing and caring for the babies, then the toddlers, then packing lunches for the school children, Tom prepared the family breakfast. No instant, drink-it-up type, it was fruit and pancakes, hot cereal, or bacon and eggs. The family loved breakfast. It was a send-off for the day. But Tom's dad was most uncomfortable with Tom's activity in the kitchen. He tried, with many subterfuges whenever he came to visit, to get Tom out of his apron and out of the kitchen. It wasn't manly, he felt. However, Tom and Abby and their children, now grown, all felt their breakfast pattern was a good one. Gran'pa, who lived in another town, did not prevail.

The children grew up and moved away, as children will. Abby's life was empty; her job had ended. Her children no longer needed her, her home did not require all her time, and the many volunteer tasks she was asked to do seemed not very meaningful after awhile. Abby wanted to do something worthwhile in the world. Her twenty years of home management were of no help to her. She couldn't even be a doctor's receptionist anymore, she said, for she was past her youth. She felt useless and unimportant, a noncontributing member of society. Life had no more zest. Even Tom was failing her. His new promotion required longer work days and he shared with her less and less of what he was doing and thinking. She had thought of taking a part-time job in a custom dress shop, but Tom had discouraged her. The people in his suburban community would think he was doing badly if his wife had to work for a seamstress.

Tom's life was also lacking in zest. For the first time in twenty years he did not hold an office in his church. He had resigned from the town's council, feeling no support from his constituency and being unwilling to join in the political chicanery. At Abby's request he had refused a promotion in his job which would have required moving out-of-state. A man with less than half his experience and years of service won the appointment. He was beginning to question the meaning of it all. He said that they would both feel better if she had allowed him to accept the promotion. She said that they would both feel better if he had allowed her to accept the job in the dress shop. Both Tom and Abby felt bad about themselves, and each of them blamed the other.

The house church listened thoughtfully while they worked through both their resentments toward and appreciation of each other. To their surprise they discovered that, in the midst of their strong feelings of resentment, they also had feelings of appreciation which they had not thought about or expressed for some time. They resented being held back by each other; they appreciated each other's caring and constancy. The leader then suggested that they ask each other for what they need.

In the end, both Tom and Abby came to feel that whatever role they worked out was right for them no matter what their parents or their children or the community felt, that each of them needed to stand on his/her own feet, be his/her own person, grow his/her own sense of self without hanging on, leaning on, or using the other. Although their roles as husband and wife are complementary, their uniqueness and individuality must not be subservient to their roles. Accordingly, Tom came to feel responsible for helping Abby develop her talents in whatever way would enable her to find a meaningful niche in society. Abby resolved that she would cease trying to find her significance through Tom's work as Tom's wife and would hang onto him less as she stood on her own feet more.

The problems of singles, couples, and families are not different from the problems of teachers, engineers, businessmen, homemakers, teen-agers. Loneliness is a fact of life for many; sorrow and grief afflicts all ages and all jobs; anger, hurt, and frustration can become part of any relationship. Life is filled with all kinds of knots for persons of every age in any situation of home, school, or work in any region of the country. We are all brothers and sisters under the skin, we all need one another's love, and that's all the house church has to give.

10. House Church Process as a Style for the Whole Church

The house church experience is not different in kind from the work and life and mission of the whole church. It is different only in degree. There is a continuum from intensive experiencing to less intensive experiencing of the Good News. Extended time, commitment, and intention enable persons in the house church to experience God, neighbor, love, and acceptance in ways not usually encountered in the total church.

The relation of the house church to the whole church can be described in several ways. It is akin to the intensive care unit of a large hospital. Not everyone wants or needs intensive care all the time, but it is available for those who do need it when they need it. The best practices, equipment, and medicines are on hand; skilled, knowledgeable, and attentive personnel are on call.

The house church can also be likened to a research and development center from which emanates information and practices which can facilitate a more vigorous life for the whole church. Or it can be thought of as a model or prototype for the whole church, or an intensive laboratory experience (like some conferences and workshops), or a learning center in which the problems and possibilities of the whole church are experienced in microcosm. House church experiencing has implications for the total life of a congregation.

A Style for the Whole Church

Two rules or ways of proceeding within the house church must become characteristic of the life of the total church if the church is to become a loving, trusting community. Sadly, many churches do not think of these rules as characteristically Christian; most churches are not completely and unfailingly able to practice them. The rules deal with the individual and the communal, that is, self-disclosure and the community response.

1. Self-disclosure means that *every person tells his own story*. No person tells (discloses) another person's story. There is no place for gossip in the Christian church.

2. A loving, communal response means *no judgment*. No one will reveal his pains or anger or mistakes if he does not feel sure that he will be unconditionally accepted. If his lovableness and worth are contingent upon the image of goodness he portrays, he is not likely to reveal anything which will tarnish his image or jeopardize his acceptance. The themes of love, acceptance, and no judgment can be found in many places in Jesus' teachings. There is a clear mandate for this way of relating to one another which is much older than the house church.

The goal of the house church, to enable the growth of love among persons (communal) and transformation from fragmentation to wholeness (individual), is also a goal of the total church. Some of the methods used in the house church can be employed with good effect in various aspects of the church's life: Sunday morning worship, board meetings, church school classes. House church methods are neither strange nor unique. In fact, they are widely used in education and in business to reduce friction and phoniness and to improve authentic relationships. It is high time the church put them to use.

It is important to recognize that self-disclosure in a total congregation cannot be and does not have to be as intensive as in many of the experiences we have described. It must only be real, personal, here and now. It can be joyous or sorrowful, hopeful or anxious, happy or hurt. No matter. An accepted and acceptable time and place where persons can share their lives and relate to one another honestly and openly is what is important. When trust grows and self-disclosure happens and love is experienced within the Christian community, the conditions exist for significant celebration, worship.

Sunday Morning Worship

One church congregation we know has built into its Sunday morning worship a "concerns of the people" time. The microphone is open to anyone who needs to share a concern with the gathered congregation. Persons thus let themselves be known to one another. Sickness, loneliness, needs, anniversaries, new jobs, political issues, protests to be made or being made, births, miscarriages, deaths, visiting relatives or friends—all these events with their feelings of anxiety, hope, disappointment, sorrow, and joy have been shared. In this particular church, the "concerns of the people" has been known to take half the time of the morning worship hour. Most of the worshipers feel that such time is more important than the sermon. In the "prayers of the people" which follows, the minister commits these many concerns to God's care. When the benediction comes and the congregation sings, "The LORD bless you and keep you: The LORD makes his face to shine upon you. . . , The LORD lift up his countenance upon you, and give you peace" they know what they are singing about and celebrating.

At the coffee hour following the service, the congregation who are aware of one another's hopes and hurts can relate to one another in caring and helpful ways. The Protestant doctrine of the priesthood of all believers thus becomes operative in ways the traditional Sunday morning worship service seldom permits.

Many other variations in the traditional Sunday morning worship can be created. Some worshipers will find them enlivening and freeing; others will feel uncomfortable and manipulated. Changes in Sunday worship which increase informality and change the focus from the historical, the objective, and the impersonal to the present time, the subjective and personal are scary changes to some. The intellectual distancing, the "head trips," the emphasis on thinking at the expense of feeling and acting make spontaneous expression of any kind suspect. When the change in the traditional and accepted order of worship can be seen as part of the style of the people of the church in all aspects of their life together, then it is not perceived as a gimmick, contrived to force a relationship, but as a real and appropriate way for people to be present to one another.

Sunday morning worship can offer individual opportunities for growth toward wholeness as well as communal opportunities for interdependent relationships. One minister used the sermon period to lead his congregation in a guided fantasy. The morning's theme was "Christian Community and the Contemporary Cry." Infinite variations on this guided fantasy can be made; the purpose of the fantasy varies little: to enable persons to confront whatever remains unfinished in their lives and to take a step in working it out. The fantasy follows:

Make yourself as comfortable as you can in these pews so that your body will not interrupt your meditation. Place your feet flat on the floor, your hands loose in your lap. Do not hold anything that will be heavy or which may slip away from you. Close your eyes and let this experience be yours alone.

In order to be aware of yourself and your body, make two fists as hard as you can, hold tight (pause), now let your hands go. Tighten your leg muscles as hard as you can, now let them go. Make a face—now let go. Breathe deeply and slowly several times.

Now, going very slowly, look around your body, inside you, and find that place where you usually feel sad or angry or fearful or glad or happy or hurt or guilty. Pay attention to that place where you carry your feelings and see who you are right now. Ask your feeling place, what is my cry as a human being today? Go slowly, let the cry come, don't force it, let it change, move around, until it feels and sounds right. Now look around your feeling place and see if any symbol or picture of your cry is there, maybe the picture of an experience out of which your cry comes. I'll give you a minute to feel and see and picture your cry.

Now in your fantasy, go to the person you would most like to share your cry with, or the person you most need to share your cry with. The person could be a friend, a family member, a stranger. It could be Jesus. Go to where you would find that person. Visualize the place, how you are sitting, what the other person looks like, and how he or she is sitting and being. Now speak to that person and tell him or her about your cry. When you finish, move over in your mind's eye and speak for the person. Respond as you imagine that person would respond. Then move back and speak again for yourself. Then be the other person again and speak for him or her. I will give you two minutes to carry on this dialogue. Pay attention to how each of you is feeling and looking as you speak.

When you have finished your dialogue, open your eyes and come back to the sanctuary.

Now I will give you five minutes to speak with one other person sitting near you. Do not, unless you wish to do so, speak about your cry or the person you spoke to in your fantasy. Speak rather about the process, what surprised you, what you became aware of in yourself.

A Board of Trustees Meeting

Deliberations about the policies and doctrines of the church in boards, committees, and church school classes can be greatly improved by the use of a few of the methods frequently employed in the house church.

1. Everyone in the group must *respond to the issue*. Go around the circle if necessary.

2. Persons must take responsibility for their position—*own their feelings*—not put them off on someone else.

3. *Check it out*. The group finds out how its own membership feels about an issue or a point of view.

Of course not all problems will be solved by the use of these three simple devices, but planning and decision-making will take place in a more honest, open, trusting climate when everyone gets his word in and straightforward, realistic conversations develop.

Consider a board of trustees meeting, for example. It is a typical Monday night meeting with ten persons present including the minister. Budget and maintenance items are dealt with as usual. Then the minister reports a request he has received for a room in the building to be used for weekly meetings of recovering drug addicts. The program is supervised by some young social workers, who are trying to build a support community for the young addicts as they attempt to make it in the community. There is a silence after the minister's presentation. He states his position that the church ought to make itself available to the community in this manner.

The trustee meetings are dominated by four persons who respond immediately.

"The congregation would probably be very divided over this issue."

"We've got to act very responsibly about this matter."

"Many people in the congregation would be frightened if they knew there were drug addicts in the church."

"We should of course try to help people like this."

"Jesus did work with sinners."

"What would happen to our furnishings and equipment?"

Several of the five silent members appear to be nodding their heads in agreement or disagreement about these statements as they are made. Finally, after half an hour of discussion the board votes to seek more data about the whole enterprise and appoints a subcommittee. The pastor leaves the meeting feeling very discouraged. The dominating members leave the meeting feeling good that they have postponed the decision, but also feeling somewhat guilty because they didn't take a stand.

How can three simple procedures improve a board meeting? First, simply going around the group, permitting and requiring everyone to make some response to the issue provides time and space for all members to get in on the act. At least each person's voice is heard. Thus the responsibility for any decision is shared and the possibility of domination by a few is reduced.

Second, requiring the members to take responsibility for their feelings rather than ascribing them to someone else (the congregation, many people, us) makes for a far more direct conversation and reduces hiddenness. Had the speaker owned his feelings, the above statements would have come out like this:

"I am divided over this issue."

"I want to be responsible about this matter."

"I would be frightened."

"I want to help."

"I want my church to respond to sinners."

"I am worried about our equipment."

Third, checking it out makes it possible for every person to find out whether anyone else in the group has the same feelings he has and what the feelings of the total group are. Had the board practiced checking it out the members would have left the meeting feeling they had been heard and that they, representing the church, could freely pursue all points of view and come up with the best answer. The board would experience something of what it means to care for one another, to be aware of how persons are feeling, to enter into reality-based communication. The exchange would not be as intensive as in an extended house church sessions, but the same fundamental style of relating would be practiced.

A Social Action Committee

For too long church persons have taken an either/or stance toward social action and personal growth. The Bible is full of protest action for justice and liberation; it is also full of requirements for personal freedom and growth. The biblical record is clear. Social action and personal growth are not alternatives; they are parts of the whole. We are called to overcome fragmentation in the person and in the community. The Christian stance is for wholeness, both in the person and in society.

The house church as the intensive care unit has some insight into this false dichotomy. The same dynamic is operating in personal stress and in social friction, namely, persons and society are fragmented and broken. They are in need of wholeness. Thus both parties are concerned about the same process. Just as the individual seeks to integrate alienated parts of himself into a more fully functioning whole, so society needs to integrate alienated and oppressed parts of itself into a more fulfilling, equitable, communal whole.

The house church process enables individual persons to do this by letting them fully experience the alienated parts of themselves, letting those parts dialogue with one another, finishing past bondages, and reintegrating unfinished experiences into a new whole. The process is dynamic and goes on for a lifetime.

Social action seeks the same goal, but achieving the goal is far more difficult in society. The whole community needs to fully experience the fragmentation, brokenness, alienation, suffering, oppression which some parts of the community feel and experience. When the parts can dialogue with one another, then some new, more fulfilling wholeness emerges.

But the blocks which do not let the parts of the community hear one another are the same primary feelings which do not allow the individual person to move beyond his fragmentation: fear, anger, hurt, guilt, and grief. These primary feelings keep the person in bondage unable to fully experience the love, the affirmation of worth, and the peace of covenantal responsibility. Social action groups are often blocked in efforts to define a position by these same frequently unexpressed individual feelings.

One house church member who had discovered that he no longer had to be afraid of fear, anger, hurt, guilt, or grief, was a member of his church's social action committee. One night the agenda included a discussion of South African apartheid and whether or not the committee should forward a resolution to the denomination recommending withdrawal of support from corporations doing business in that country. Resource persons for the evening included two South African graduate students and two black churchmen from the city.

The blacks were unanimous and outspoken in their views that the church ought to use its influence and resources to protest racial policies in Africa. The social action committee's division of opinion became more pronounced as the discussion progressed. Finally, there were two defensive positions being politely hurled around the room: the blacks and part of the committee versus the conservative members who opposed the committee's taking any stand. The meeting appeared deadlocked, when someone asked one of the South Africans, "When are you returning to your homeland?"

He hesitated before responding and then in a quiet tone of voice said, "I'm not sure. . . I'm not sure what it will be like."

Another committee member: "Are you afraid to go back?"

South African: "Well, no. . . well, kind of."

Committee member: "What are you afraid of?"

South African: "I'm not sure."

At this point many persons appeared restless and somewhat embarrassed, but the house church member knew about fear and how it immobilizes people. He said, "It's all right to be afraid. I've been afraid many times. I would be helped and honored if you could share your fear with us."

The South African looked around the group, then back at the house church member, and then he said with considerable emotion, "I'm afraid of dying."

The committee members looked even more embarrassed, but the house church member felt more and more at home. "Tell us about that."

The South African began talking about facing the possibility of death at his young age because of his Christian views; the blacks told of their fear of death on American streets; the white, middle-class American committee members agreed that fear of death was something shared by everyone in the room. One of the blacks put the issue straight. "Until a man has faced his own death, he is not free to live."

Rather abruptly, the discussion of the social action committee had changed from defensive debate to an important sharing of what everyone in the room had in common, feelings about death.

Just before a very late adjournment time, the social action committee resolved.to continue the discussion of the denomination's stand vis-á-vis South Africa the very next week. What had begun as an intellectual battle of wits and ideological positions ended as a mutual human search for abundant life for *all* persons, those in the church parlor and those in South Africa's streets.

If individuals and society are plagued by the same fragmentation, and the process for finding new wholeness is the same, then church persons interested in personal growth and social action have everything in common. The church's true concern is not either personal growth or social action. It is both.

Utilizing the house church style throughout the life of the church will increasingly become second nature as church men and women gain skill in the practice of love. Innovations in traditional forms and practices are limited only by imagination. Hence church members will find themselves increasingly inventive as they relate their house church style of behaving to their other relationships in the church and the community.

Church School Classes

Church school classes can adapt various methods of the house church process to classroom experience. A teacher of an adult Bible class, having experienced a complete turnaround in his personal life as a result of a house church weekend, proposed a two-chair dialogue as a method of discovering meaning in the parables. He suggested that the class members choose any parable which intrigued them, read it, and then play it out before the class. The parable thus became a kind of guided fantasy. Each person revealed to himself, as much as to his fellow Christians his stuck point, that is, where he was troubled, confused, or ambivalent.

A class member volunteered using the familiar parable of the laborers in the vineyard (Matt. 20:1–16). He was given several empty chairs in the middle of the class circle, and he played the parts of the owner, the steward, and the men who came at different hours and received equal pay. At first he acted the parts very much according to the biblical story, but as he got into the parts he began to improvise and to be the first-hour man complaining to the steward, then the steward answering, and finally the steward taking up the dispute with the owner. He was enjoying himself. He said that he knew that the owner was right, men should be paid according to their need, but it just seemed unfair that everyone got the same wage.

The teacher asked him to be the first-hour man and the eleventh-hour man and carry on a dialogue by sitting alternately in two chairs representing these men. He did this.

First-hour man: "I feel like I've been cheated. I worked all day, and I earned just as much as you did. And you only worked one hour. I'm angry about that."

Eleventh-hour man: "But I need just as much money as you do to clothe and feed my family. I'm just as needy as you are."

First-hour man: "But it's not fair. I worked so hard and so much longer."

Eleventh-hour man: "I didn't make *your* contract, I only made mine. I agree with you that it seems unfair. You *have* worked hard, and I appreciate that. Your long hours of labor have made mine lighter."

The man stopped the drama abruptly. His voice grew husky as he said, "I've just realized something. I have always felt that injustice and uncaring were what that parable is all about. I've always seen myself as working hard, starting early, and stopping late, and no one seemed to care. I've been trying to secure my salvation through works. The works may not be sufficient but, to my astonishment, my fellow workers *do* appreciate me."

He sat down, obviously moved. In the discussion which followed, men and women discussed work and pay and hours and justice and union contracts and inflation and *doing* versus *being*. Although the work issues appeared to have no single solution, individual persons found some new integration of their frag- mented selves.

In another class it was discovered that many persons do not speak out in class because they are afraid they will be wrong. (Although this was a class of adults, children are also afraid of being wrong.) The class adopted the house church ground rules. "Receive persons (and what they offer) without judgment and without interpretation." It took some weeks, but the class climate gradually became more accepting and trustworthy as the members realized that they would no longer be denigrated, put down, or ignored by the teacher or other class members. Some of the ideas were debated and challenged, but none were treated as not worthy of consideration.

A recurrent discussion in this class was about conflict. How could a Christian resolve conflict? What attitude should a Chris- tian take toward his neighbor with whom he disagrees? Maria suggested dialogue as she had experienced it in the house church as a way of putting an issue before the class.

Joe, who was particularly vocal and aggressive about his con- servative stance politically, could not understand anyone who voted liberal, (which usually meant Democratic in that town). Yet he acknowledged that he would like to understand some of his liberal friends better.

It was at this point that Maria suggested the dialogue, and he agreed to try it. Two chairs were set out. He took his chair as Mr. X and with great gusto said, "Mr. Y, you are dead wrong about these issues. The sooner the government stops controlling things the better off we will be. You and I have argued about this for a long time, and I'm not convinced. Now you are advocating national health insurance. That's ridiculous." There was a sil- ence, and the group encouraged him to move to Mr. Y's chair to respond.

More silence. Then softly Joe said to no one in particular that this was harder than he expected; no it was easy, but he didn't

know whether he wanted to say these things for Mr. Y. Then he
spoke.

Mr. Y: "Mr. X, you don't listen to me. I've told you a hundred
times about the need for health care in some of the poorer
neighborhoods and the lack of resources to pay for that
care. How do you propose to meet that need?"

Mr. X (back in his own chair): "I think there are better ways to
do it without getting a huge bureaucracy set up which will
be wasteful. I saw too much of that kind of waste during
the war."

Mr. Y: "I'm willing to talk about alternatives, but you always
just go off on a speech on bureaucracy. We never really
talk."

Joe (looking at the class members): "This is a powerful
method. I've learned about as much as I can for one
morning. I'm going home and listen to Mr. Y for once
and see what happens."

Some weeks later the class invented a further dialogic part
when it encountered conflict. One day when a person was playing
out the two-chair dialogue and nothing seemed to be happening, a
class member suggested that a third chair be added, God's chair.
She said that God is often part of a Christian's internal dialogues.
The person in conflict agreed. His dialogue went on, but he did
not sit in God's seat or speak for God. Finally, the class pressed
him to sit in God's chair. He went over and began to sit down,
almost touching the seat. Suddenly he jumped up and moved
away. What happened? "I know what God is going to say, and I
don't want to hear it," he said. Everyone laughed. He went on to
say that he became aware that neither of the alternatives of his
conflicted self were in keeping with God's commandment.

The goals of the house church (sometimes thought of as the
little church inside the big church) are the same as for the institutional church. The number of hours spent at one time and the
commitment of the members to follow an agenda arising from the
personal concerns of one anothers' lives make the house church
different. It becomes a place where persons put together their

fragmented selves and their broken relationships. In the process, they learn skills and ways of behaving which are valuable to the total congregation. Love, fear, anger, and pain are universal; ambivalences, fragmentations, and estrangements are disabling, acceptance, forgiveness, and reconciliation are longings of the human spirit no matter what its age, sex, or condition. The process, the style, the ways of listening, caring, responding can become part of the daily life of the persons in the pews. When it does, the total church—indeed, the entire society—will reveal the honest love of God through the practice of an authentic love of persons.

Selected References

1. Allen, Donald. *Barefoot in the Church*. Richmond: John Knox Press, 1972. All about a variety of contemporary church experiences.
2. Anderson, Phil. *Church Meetings That Matter*. Philadelphia: United Church Press, 1965. Group dynamics in the life of the church.
3. Bach, George R., and Wyden, Peter. *The Intimate Enemy*. New York: William Morrow & Co., 1969. How to fight fair in love and marriage with specific illustrations.
4. Bernard, Jessie. *The Future of Marriage*. New York: World Publishing Co., 1972. With considerable documentation, Dr. Bernard shows that every marriage is composed of his marriage and her marriage; the two are not the same.

5. Clinebell, Charlotte H. *Meet Me in the Middle*. New York: Harper & Row, 1973. A clear picture of the changing roles of husband and wife and a proposal of a style of marriage that will hold together in the face of changes.

6. Clinebell, Howard. *The People Dynamic*. New York: Harper & Row, 1972. Changing self and society through growth groups with particular reference to church groups.

7. Clinebell, Howard, and Clinebell, Charlotte. *Intimate Marriage*. New York: Harper & Row, 1970. A down-to-earth understanding of marriage and ways to achieve or enhance its growth. An excellent book especially for persons who have no support group.

8. Egan, Gerard. *Encounter*. Belmont, Calif.: Brooks/Cole Pub., 1970. Thorough summary of encounter group movement. Special reference to contract development in groups.

9. Fagan, Joel, and Shepherd, Irma Lee. *Gestalt Therapy Now*. Palo Alto, Calif.: Science and Behavior Books, 1970. An excellent introduction to the methods and philosophy of Gestalt therapy.

10. Furnish, Victor Paul. *The Love Command in the New Testament*. Nashville: Abingdon Press, 1972. A scholarly support for the love ethic as the base of the earliest church and the church today. The place and time for obedience in love are always here and now.

11. James, Muriel. *Born to Love*. Reading, Mass.: Addison-Wesley Publishing Co., Inc., 1973. An analysis of and proposals for the life of the church using concepts of transactional analysis.

12. James, Muriel, and Ingeward, Dorothy. *Born to Win*. Reading, Mass.: Addison-Wesley Publishing Co., Inc., 1971. Transactional analysis and Gestalt methods for increasing personal awareness, self-responsibility, and genuineness.

13. Jourard, Sidney. *The Transparent Self*. New York: Van Nostrand Reinhold Co., 1971. Self-disclosure as the key in human relationships.

14. Jud, Gerald, and Jud, Elisabeth. *Training in the Art of Loving*. Philadelphia: United Church Press, 1972. The church and the human potential movement experienced and researched in shalom retreats.

15. Leslie, Robert. *Sharing Groups in the Church*. Nashville: Abingdon Press, 1971. Specific guidelines, many case studies, and examples for the development and clearly structured activity of sharing groups in the church.

16. Oden, Thomas. *The Intensive Group Experience*. Philadelphia: The Westminster Press, 1972. A comparison of secular encounter experience with small group life in the history of the church, e.g., Wesleyan groups, etc.

17. Olsen, Charles. *The Base Church*. Atlanta, Ga.: Forum, 1973. A
    statement of various kinds of groups in the church. *Creating
    Community Through Multiple Forms* is the subtitle of this book.
18. Stevens, John O. *Awareness*. New York: Bantom Books, 1973.
    Experiments based on Gestalt therapy to increase one's own sen-
    sitivity and awareness and to deepen relationships.
19. House Church issues in the *Chicago Theological Seminary Register*
    (December 1970), vol. 61, see "A Short Summary and Some
    Long Predictions" by Eugene Gendlin about the need for indi-
    vidual and small group belonging in our culture; (February 1973),
    vol. 63, see "Experience as a Datum of Theology" by Perry
    LeFevre; (November 1973), vol. 64, see especially four confer-
    ence papers about experience in local churches across the country.